▲ ART THERAPY COLORING

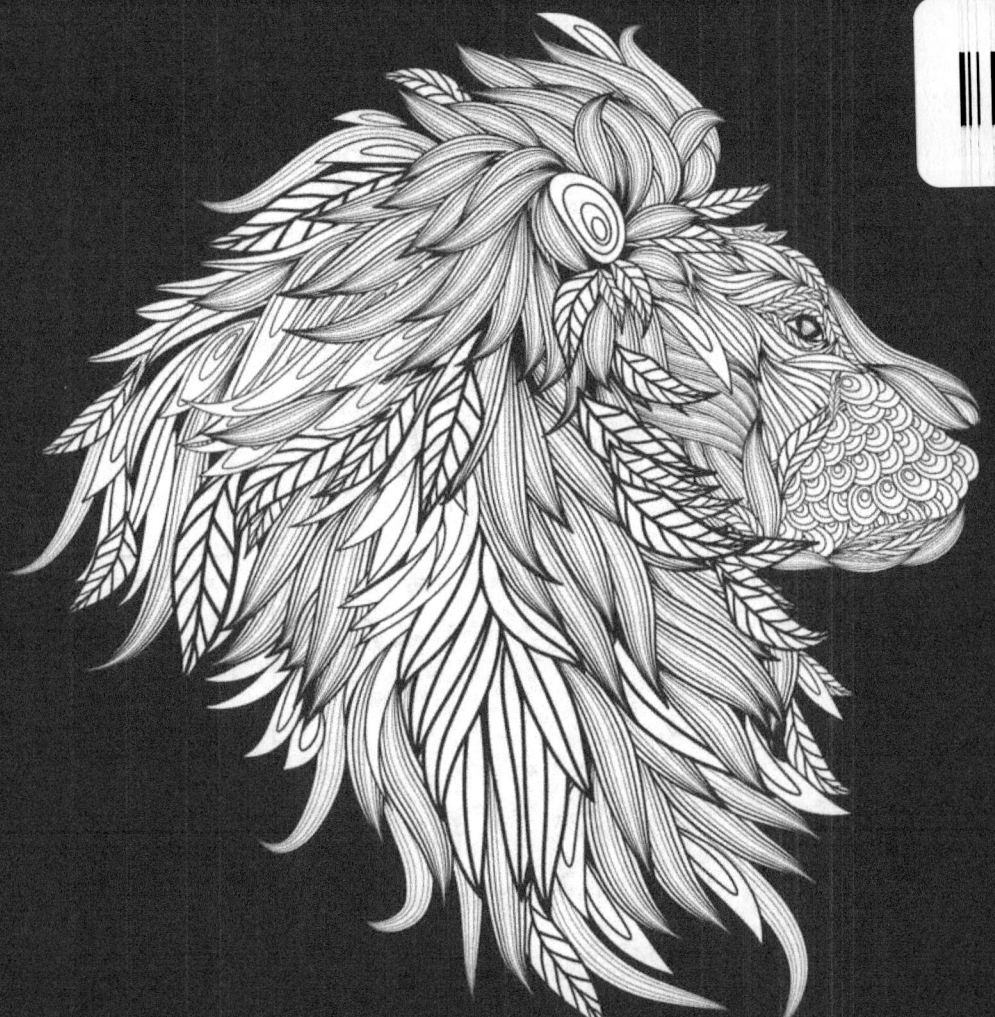

INTRICATE
COLORING BOOK
FOR ADULTS VOL 3

Preview of Coloring Pages

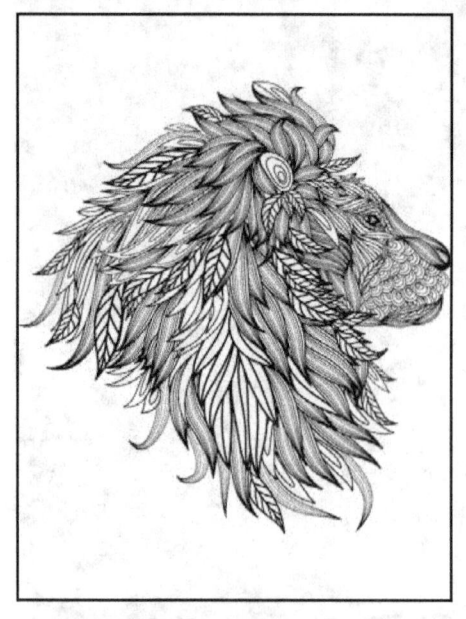
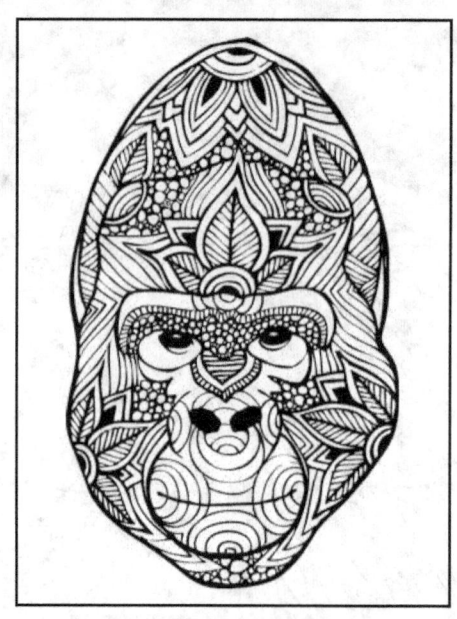
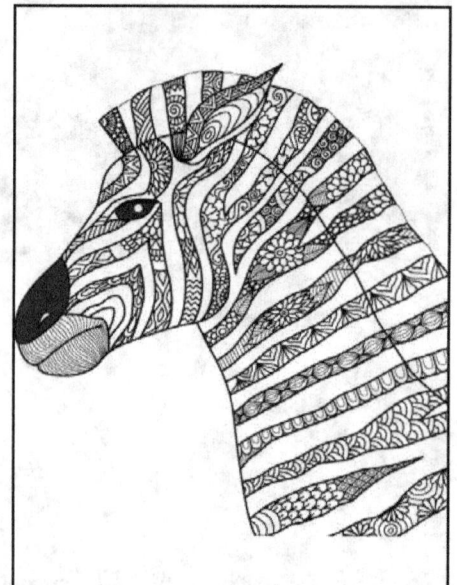
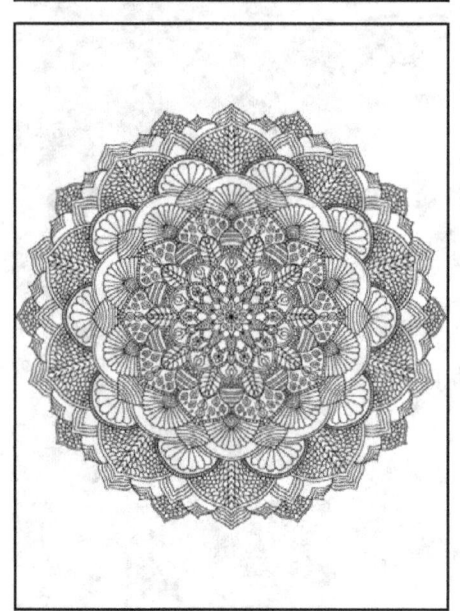
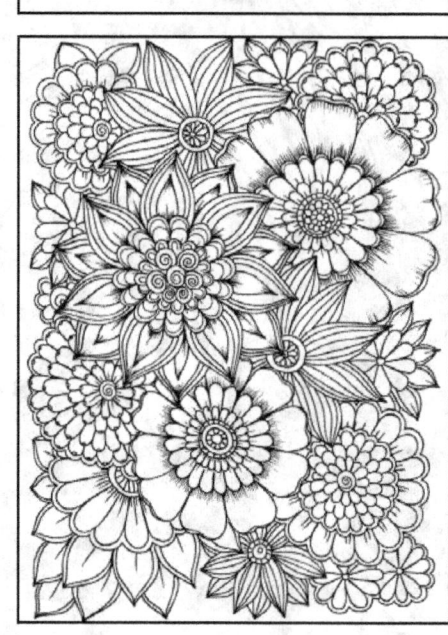
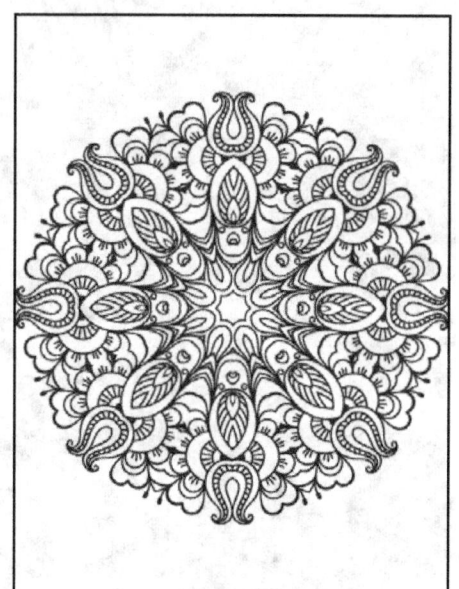
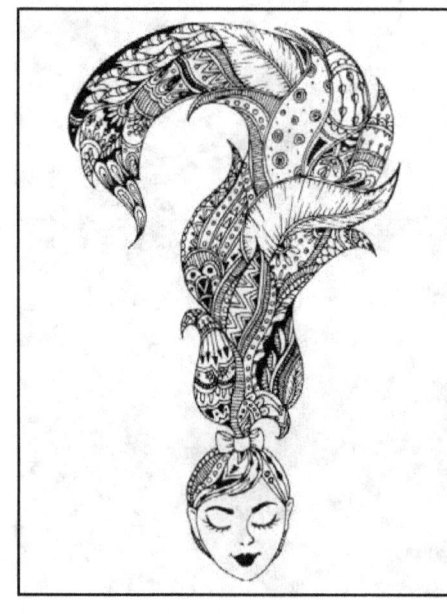
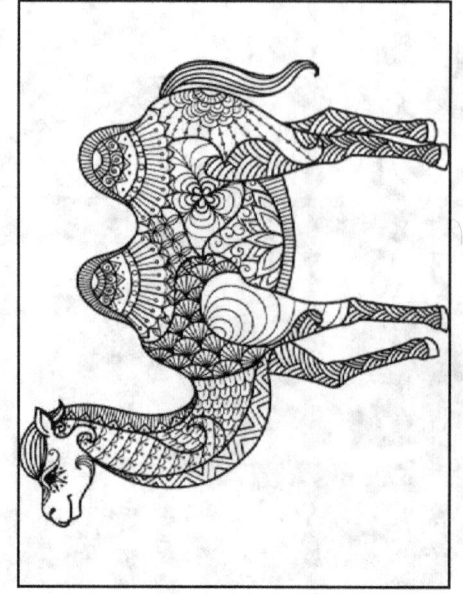
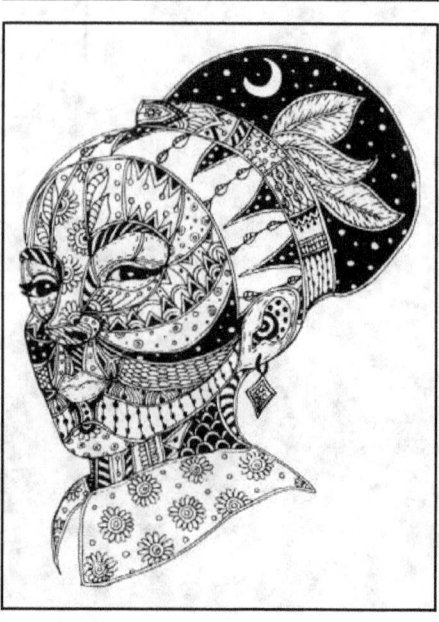

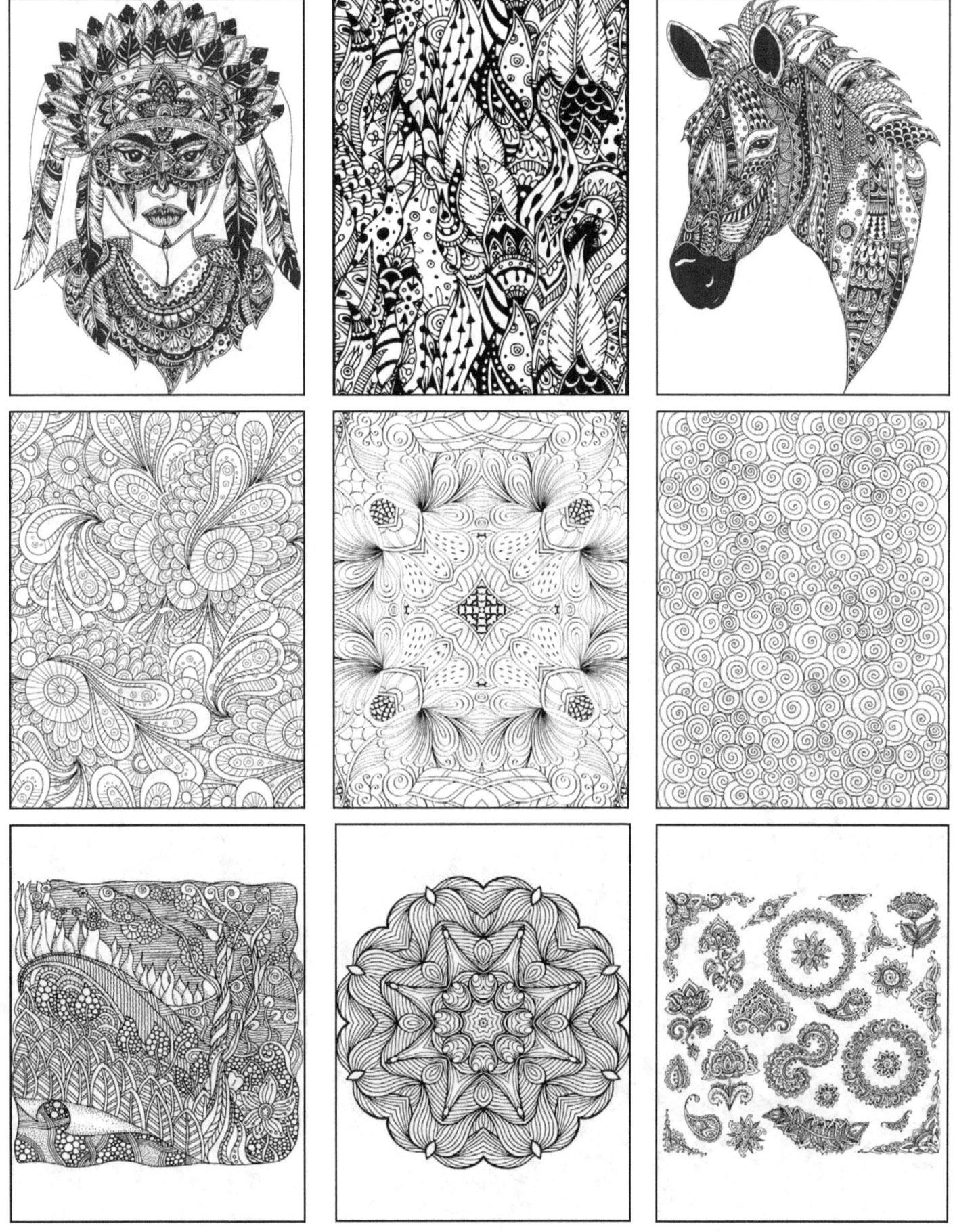

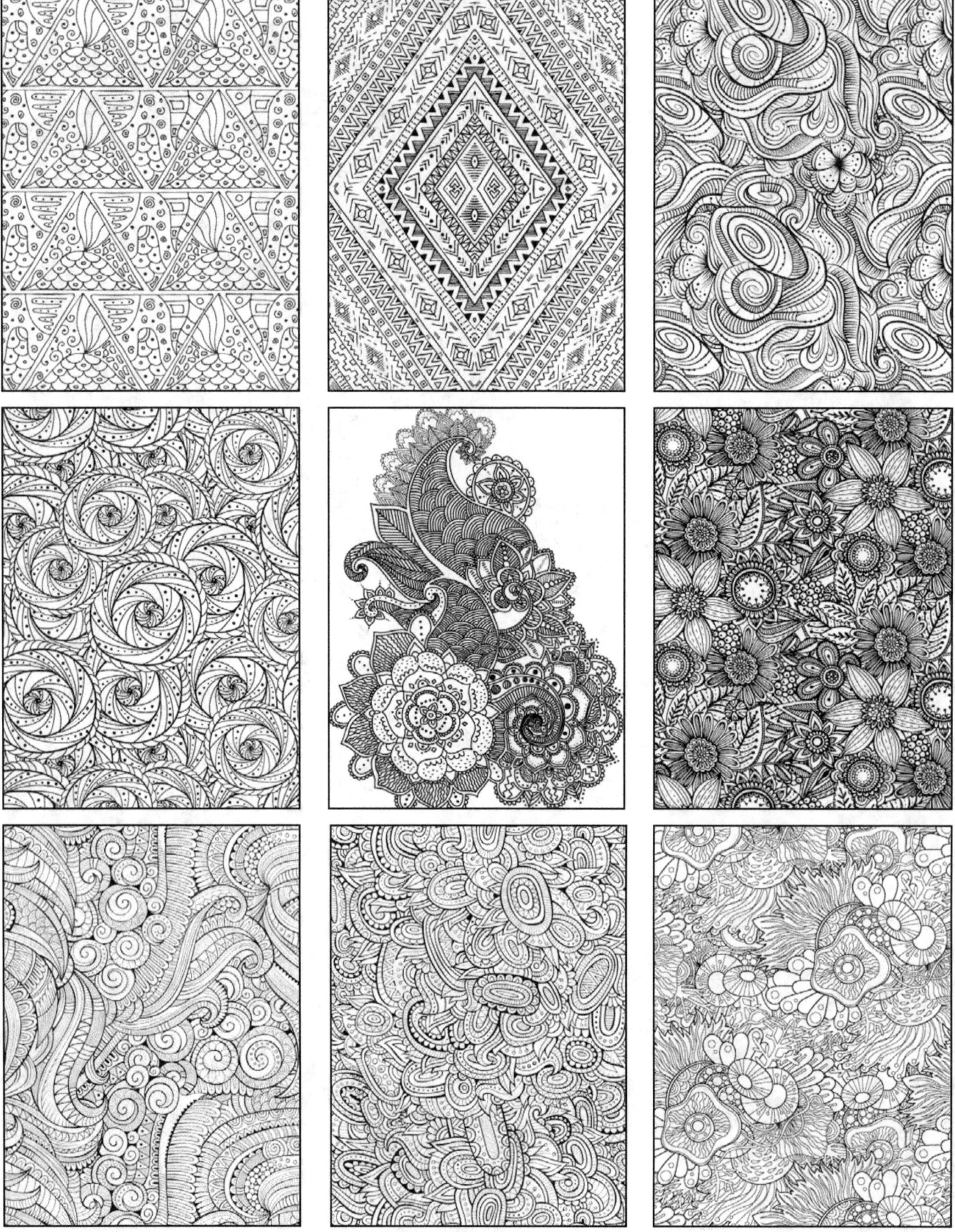

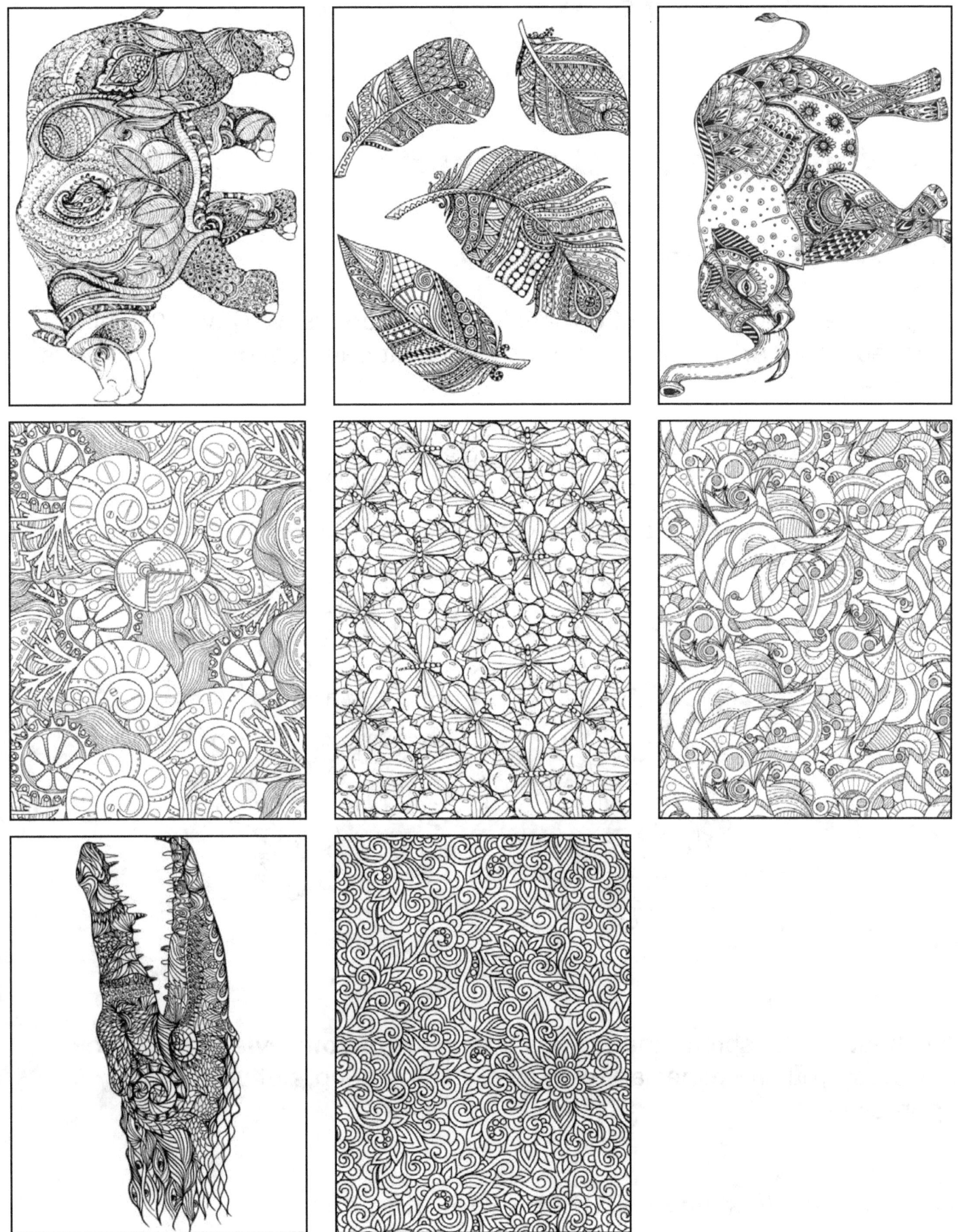

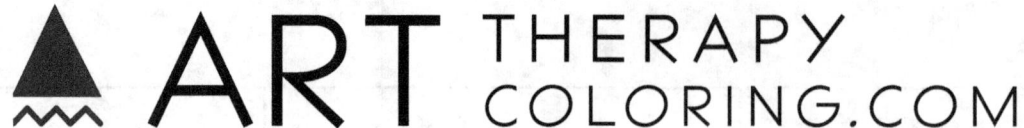

Did You Enjoy Our Coloring Book?

We Want To Hear About It!

Help spread the word about our adult coloring books! We give 10% of all proceeds from Art Therapy products to benefit pancreatic cancer patients and their families.

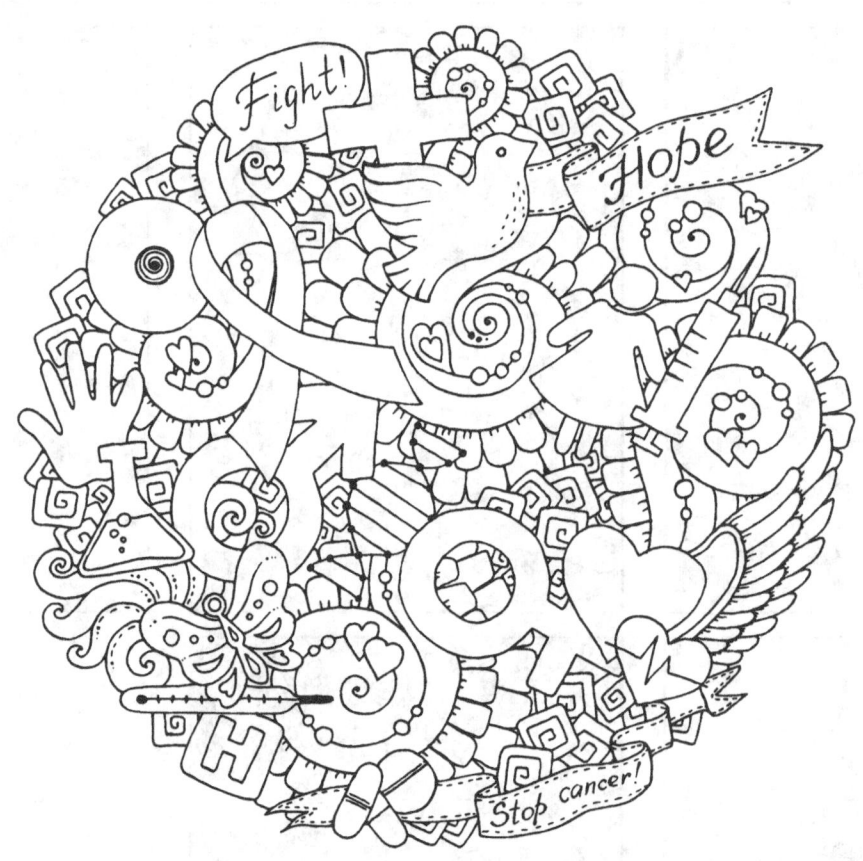

The best way to spread the word is through **Amazon reviews**. We know how busy you are, especially with all of that coloring, but we would appreciate it!

Visit our website at **www.arttherapycoloring.com**

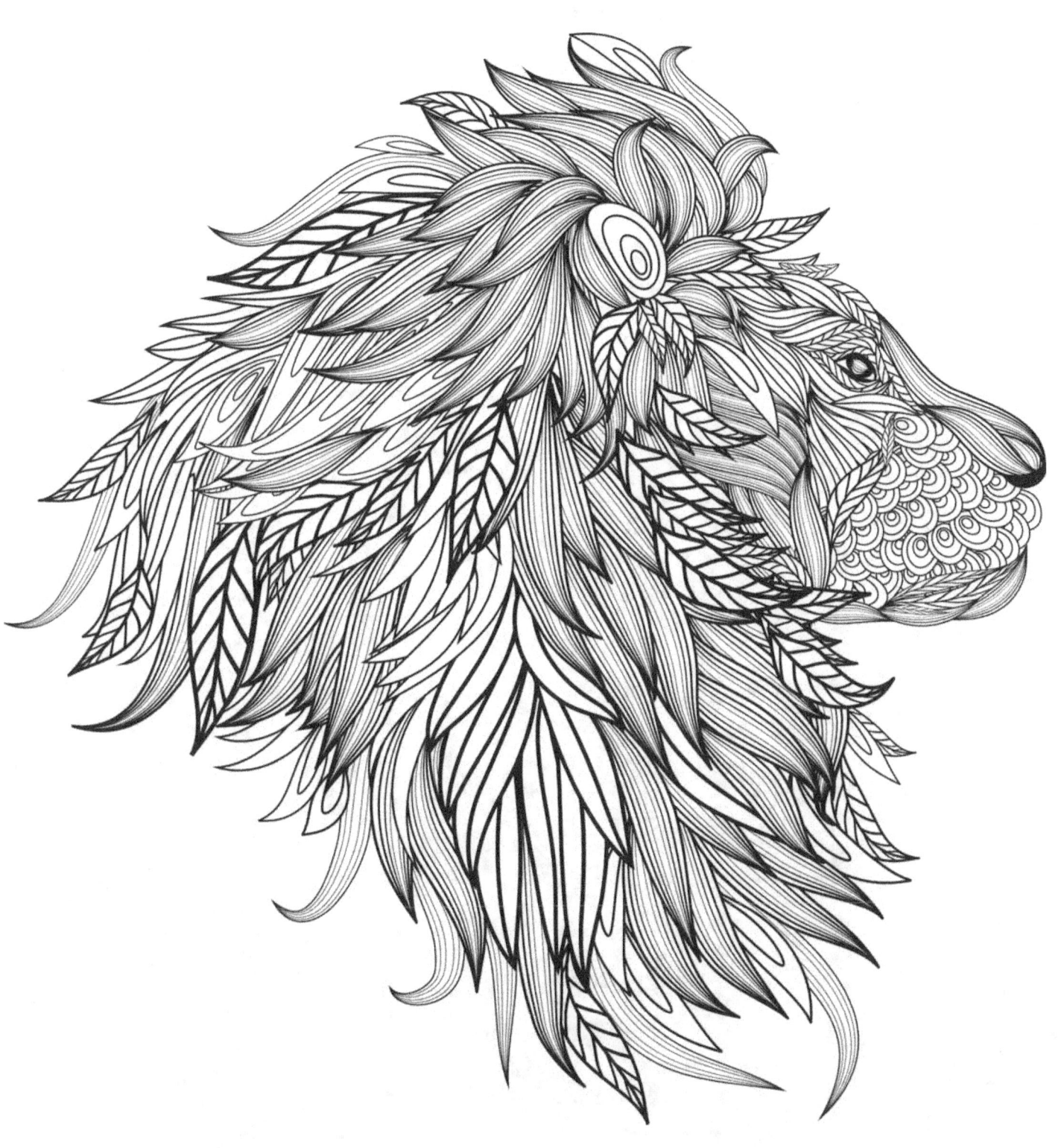

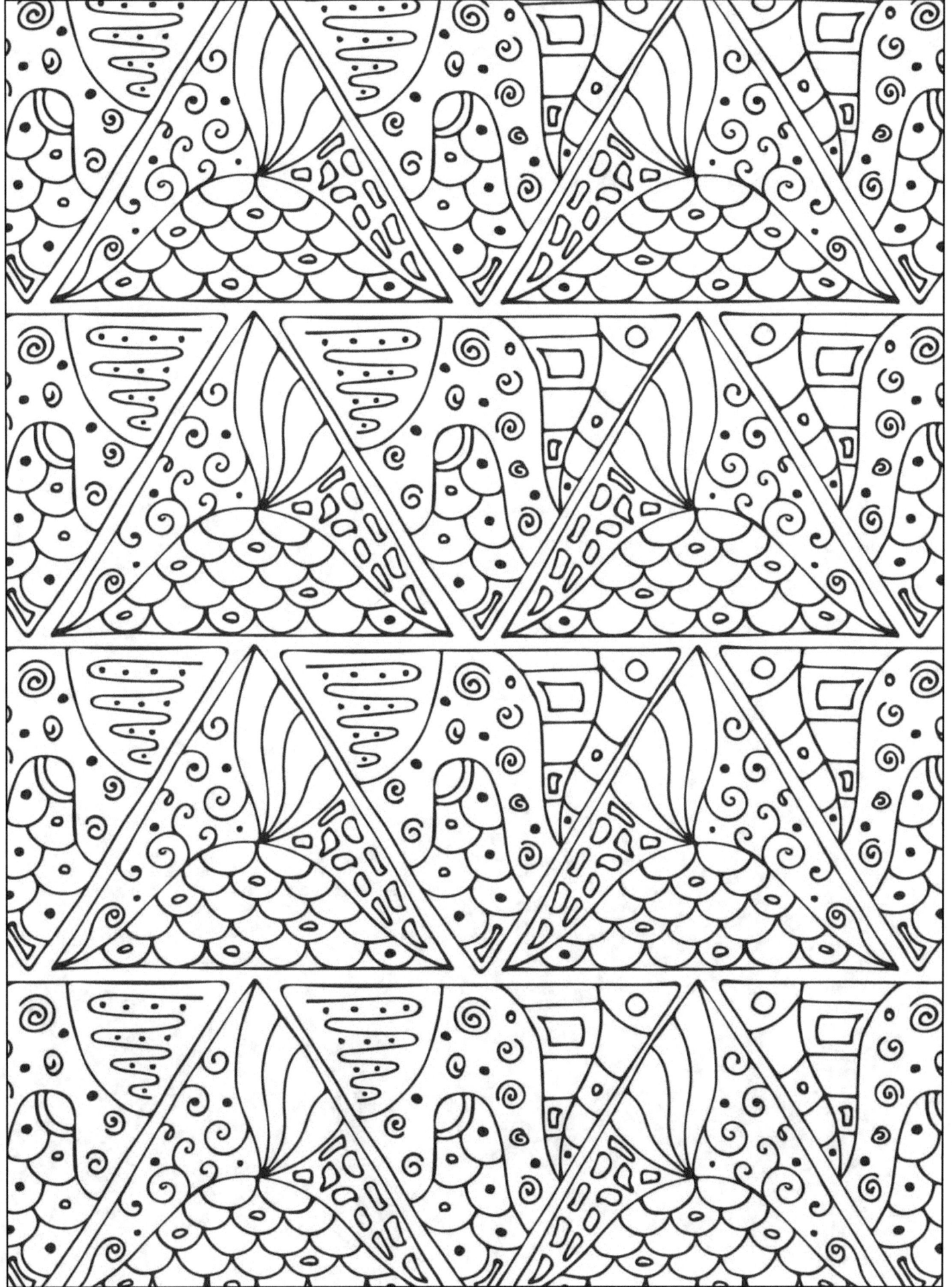

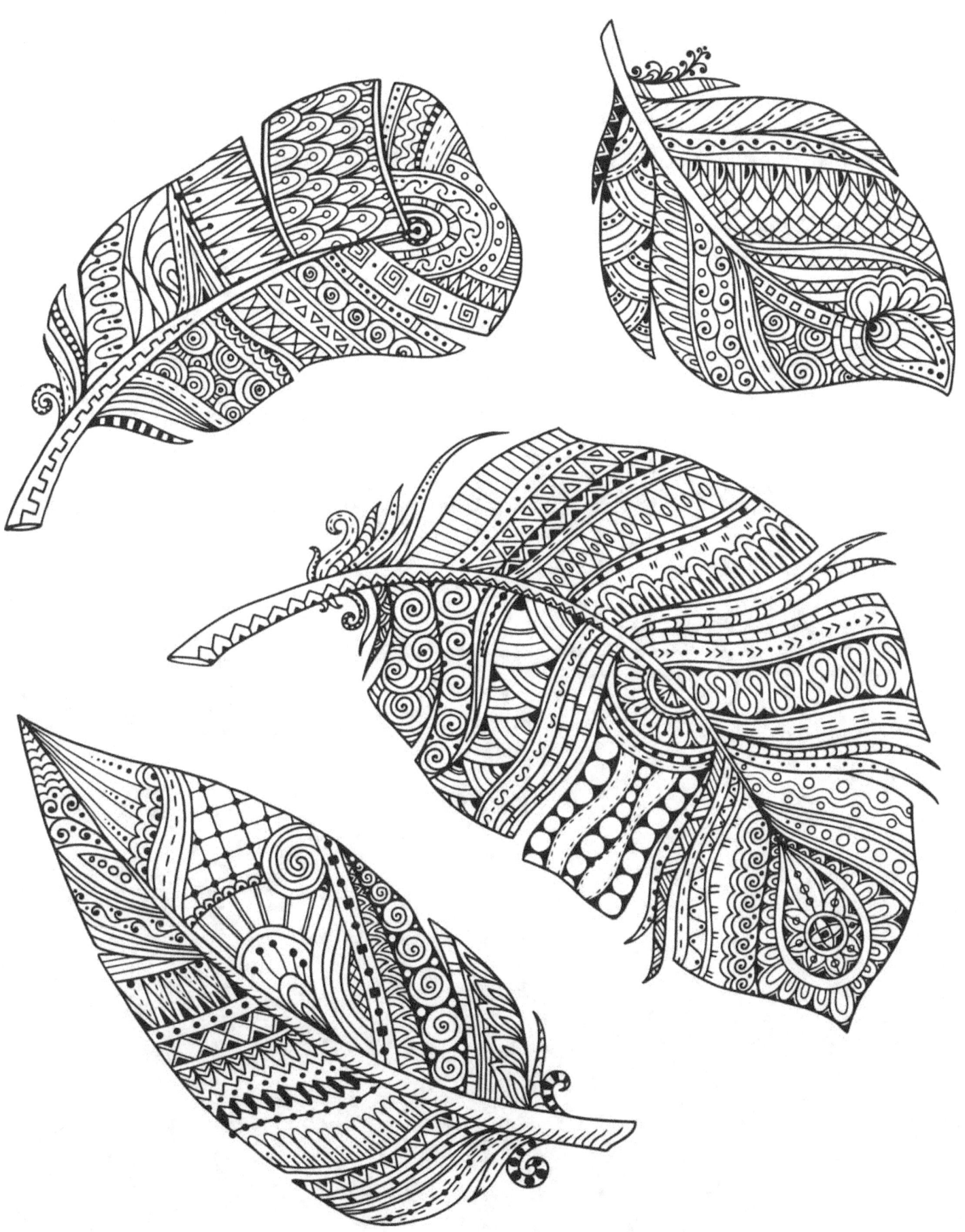

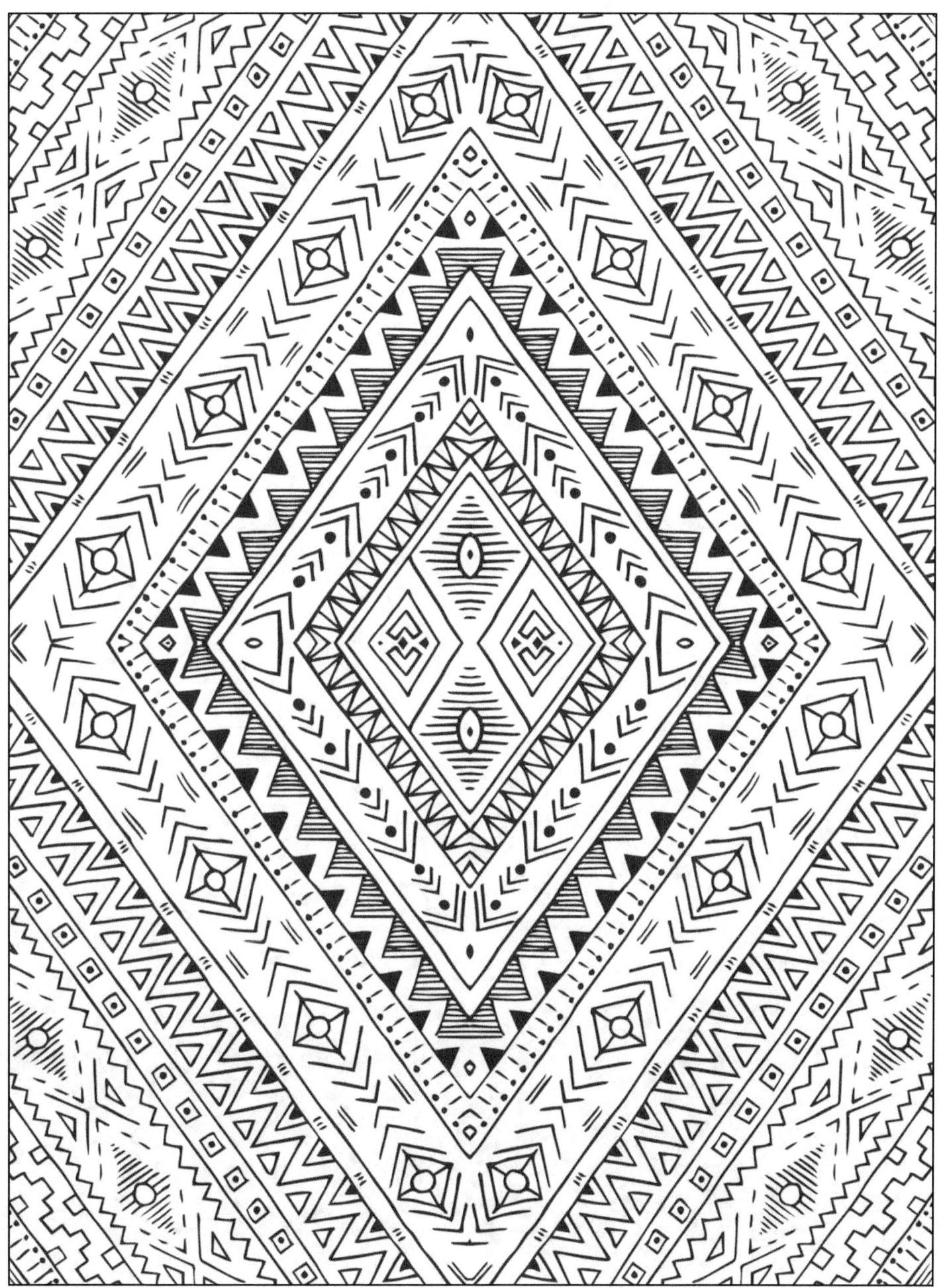

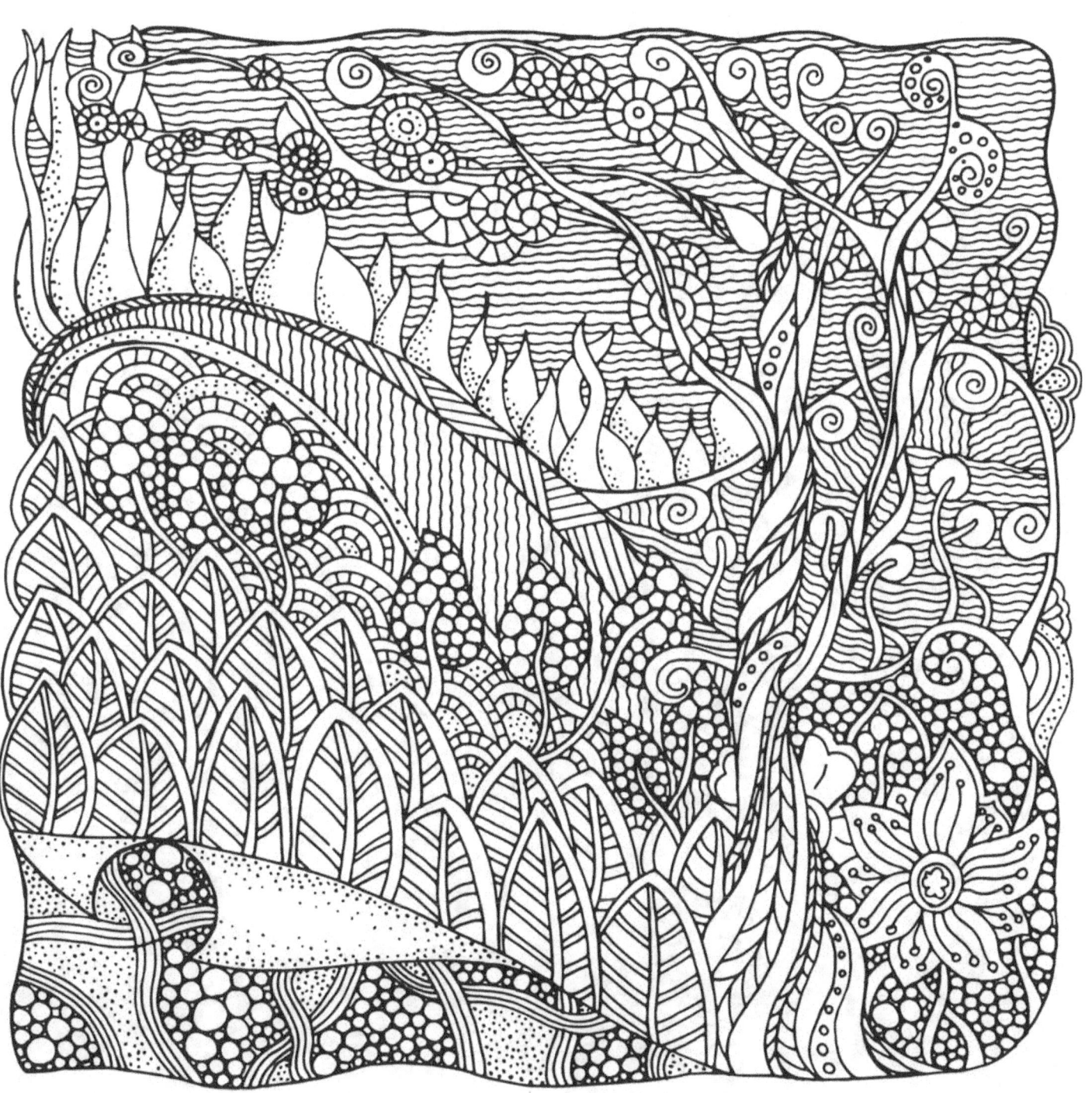

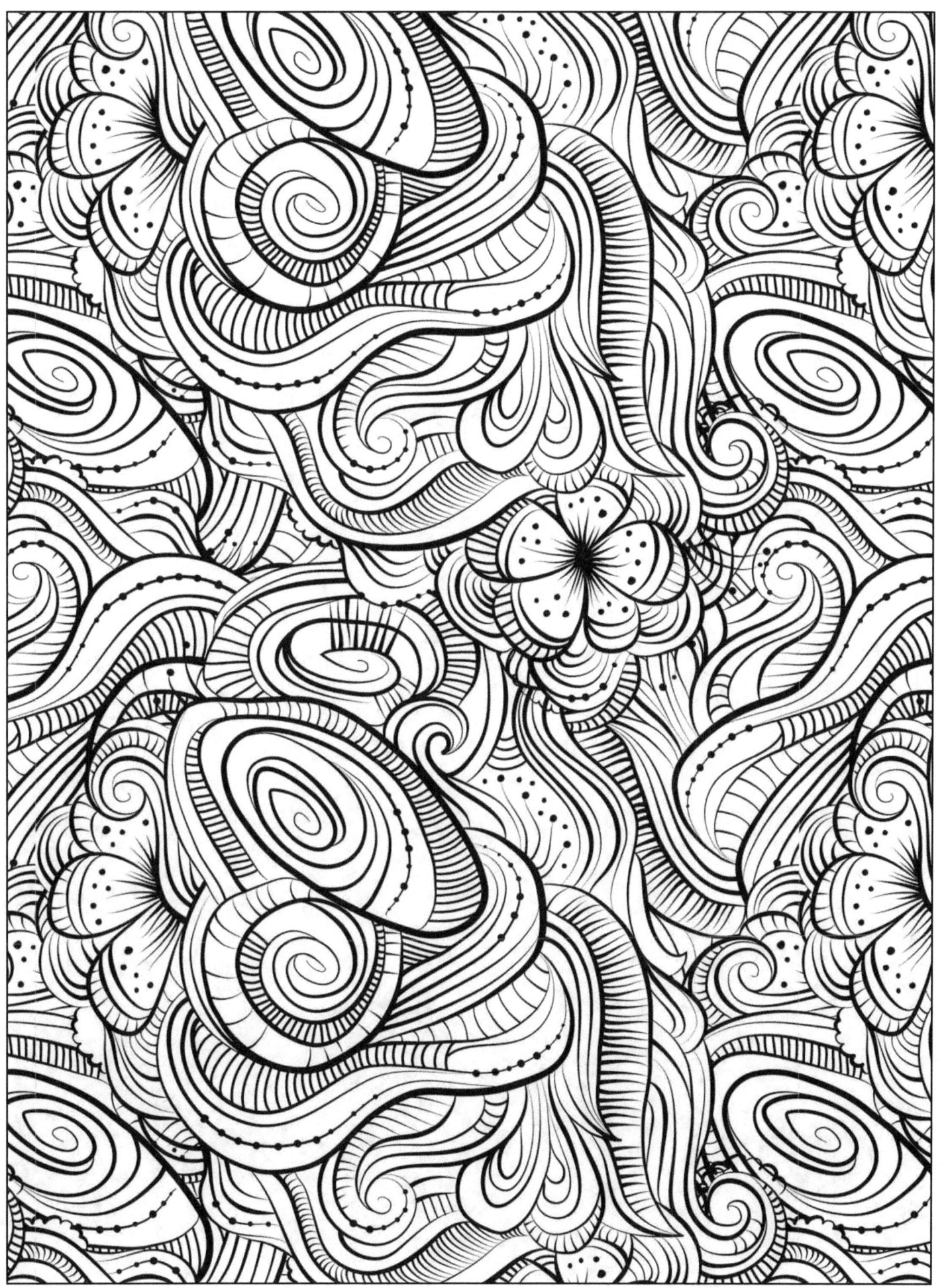

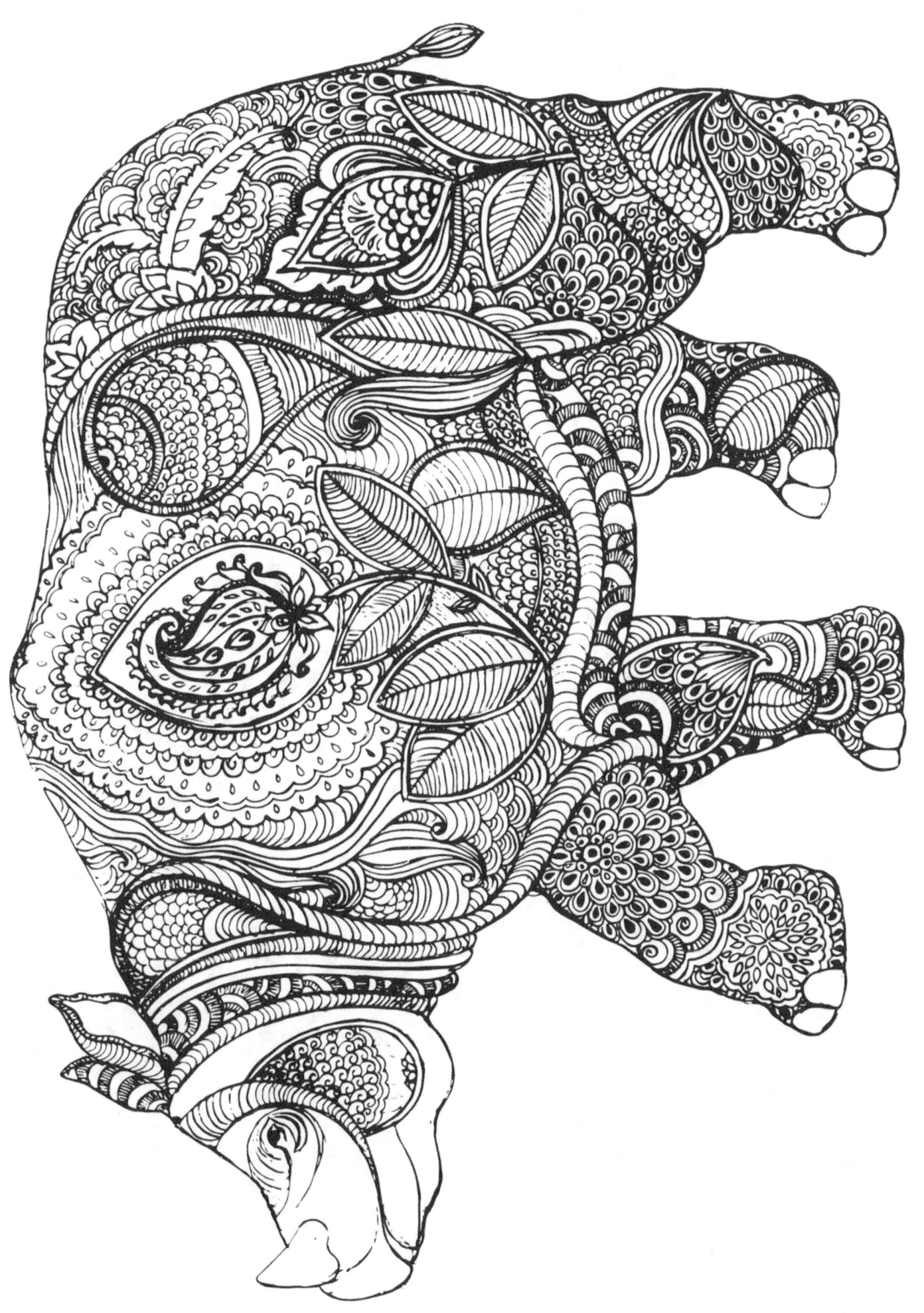

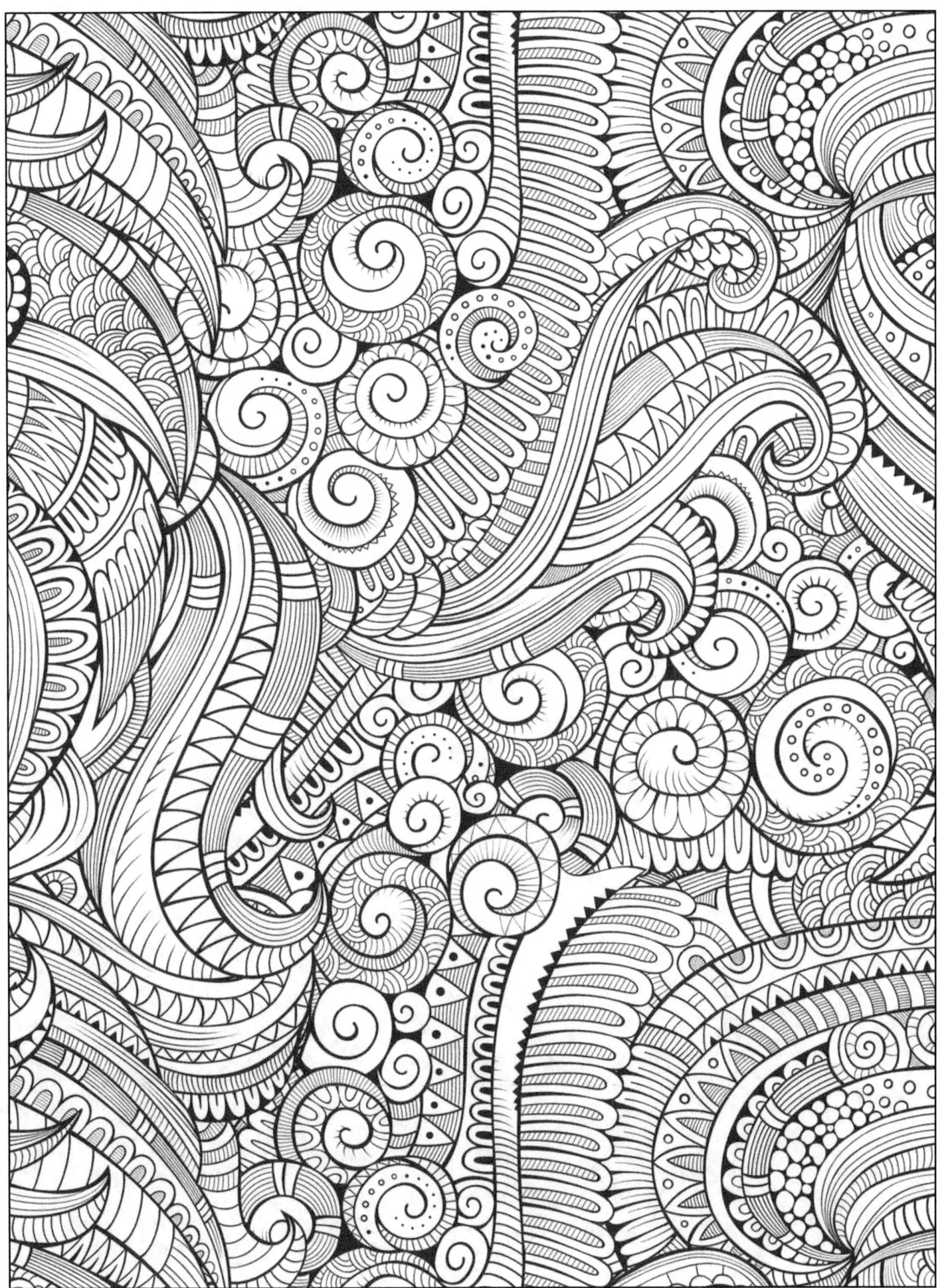

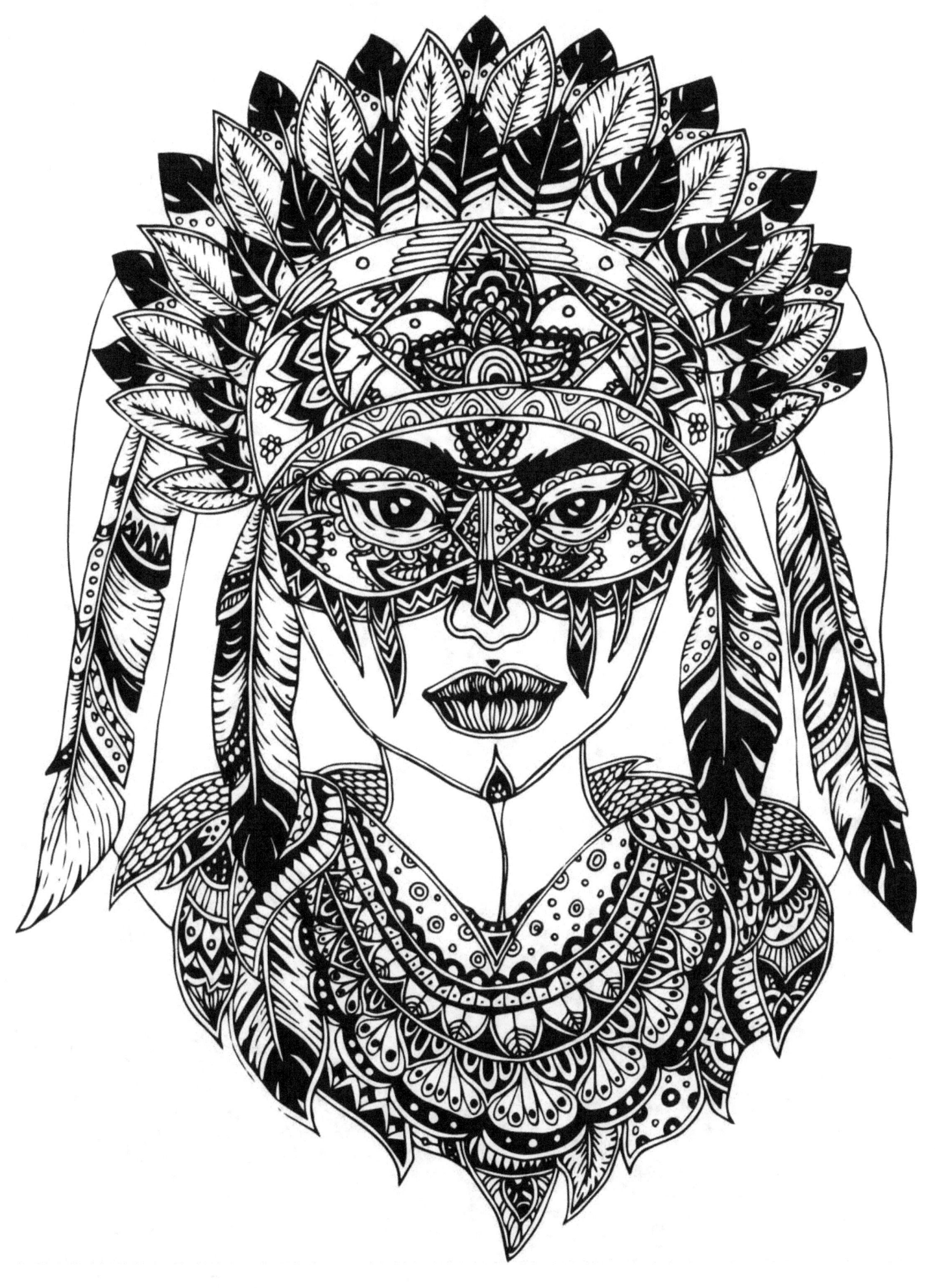

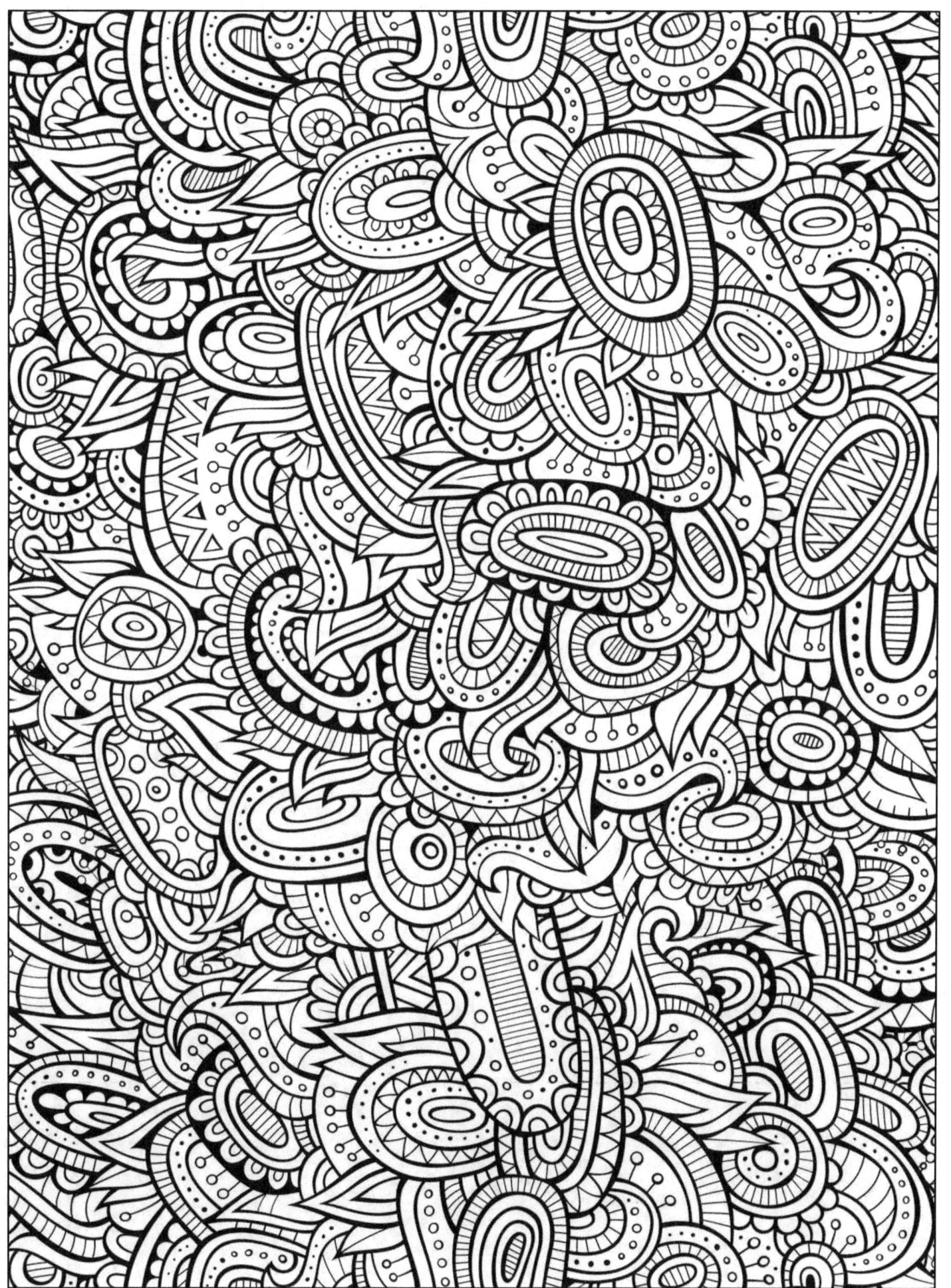

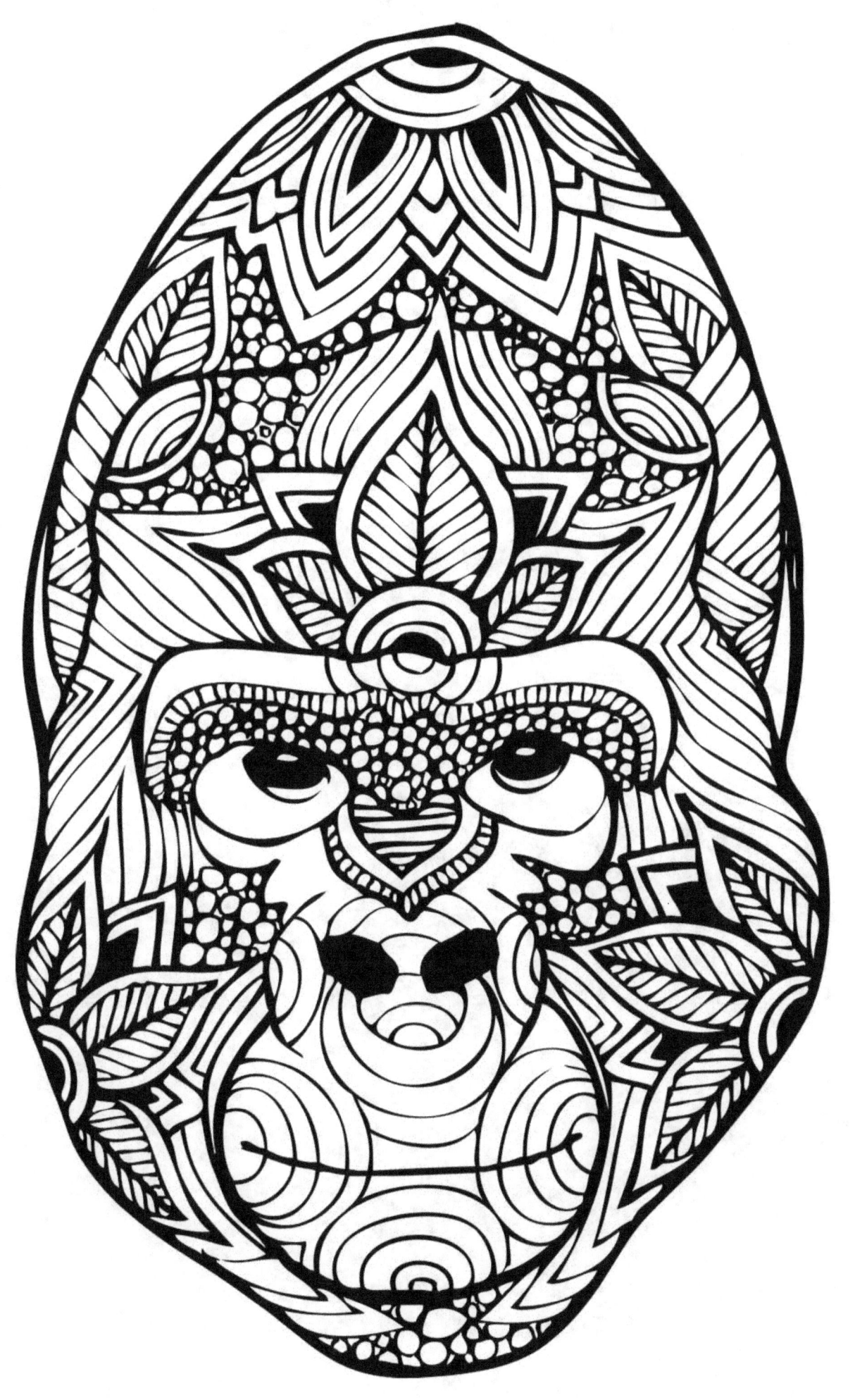

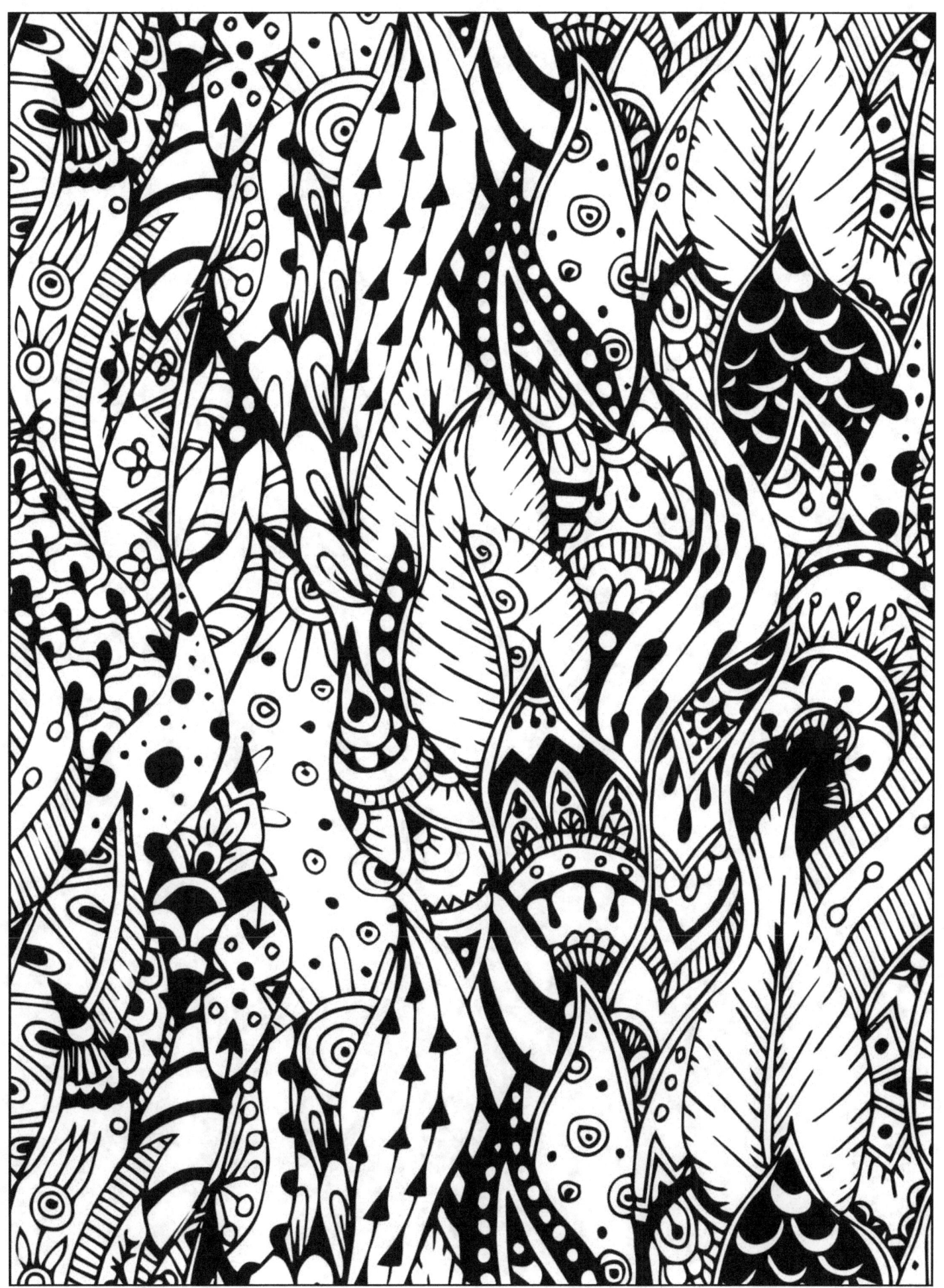

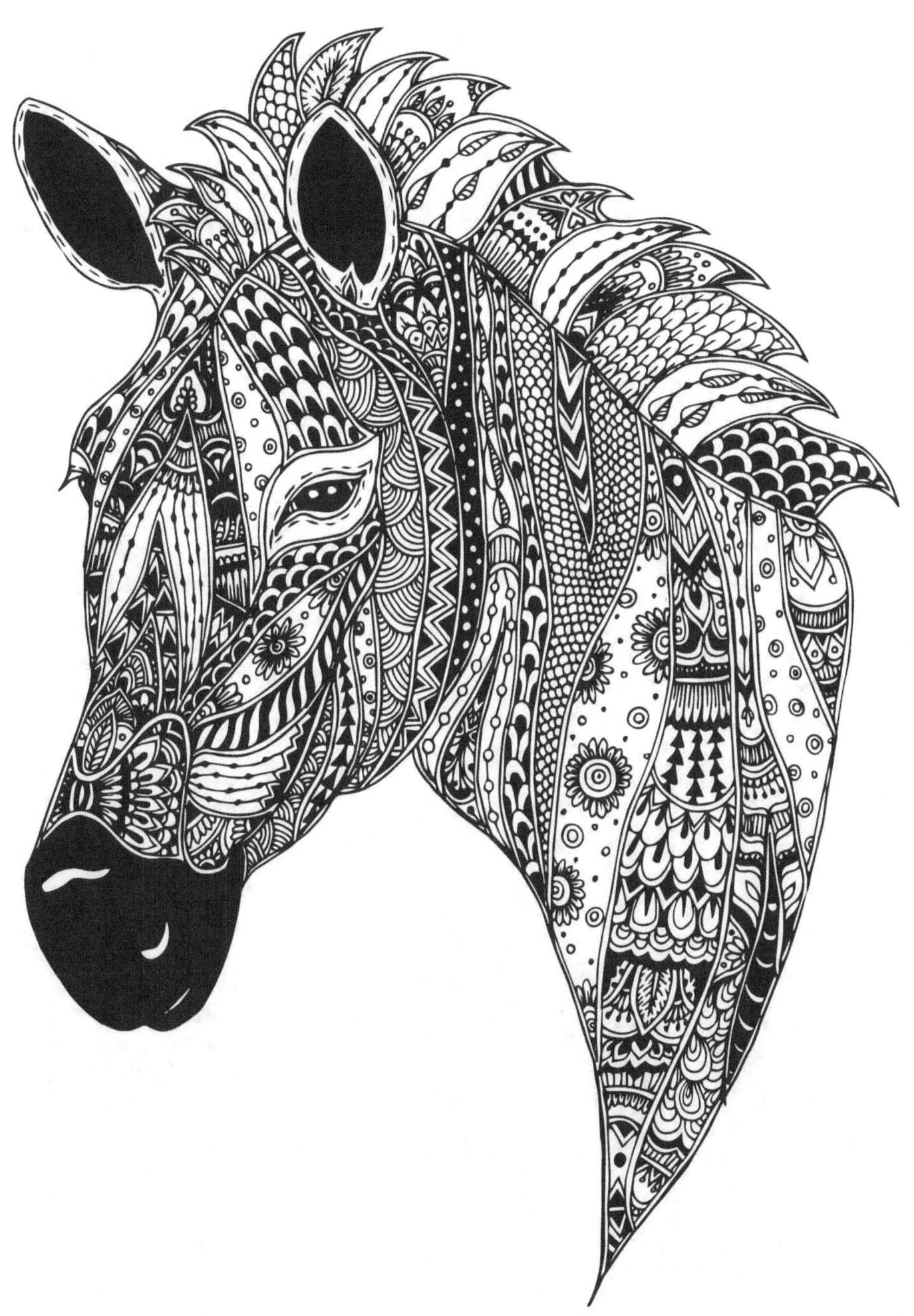

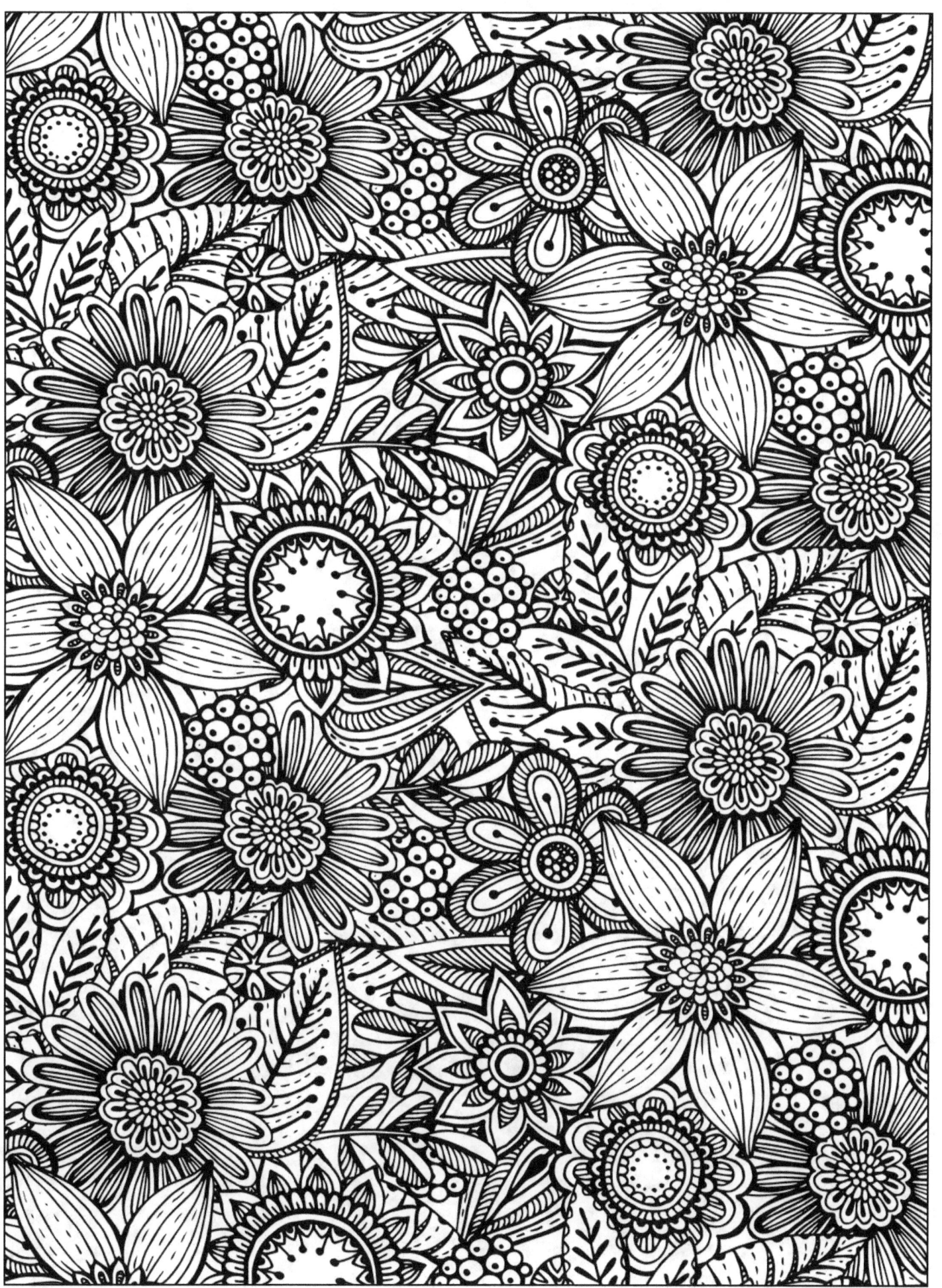

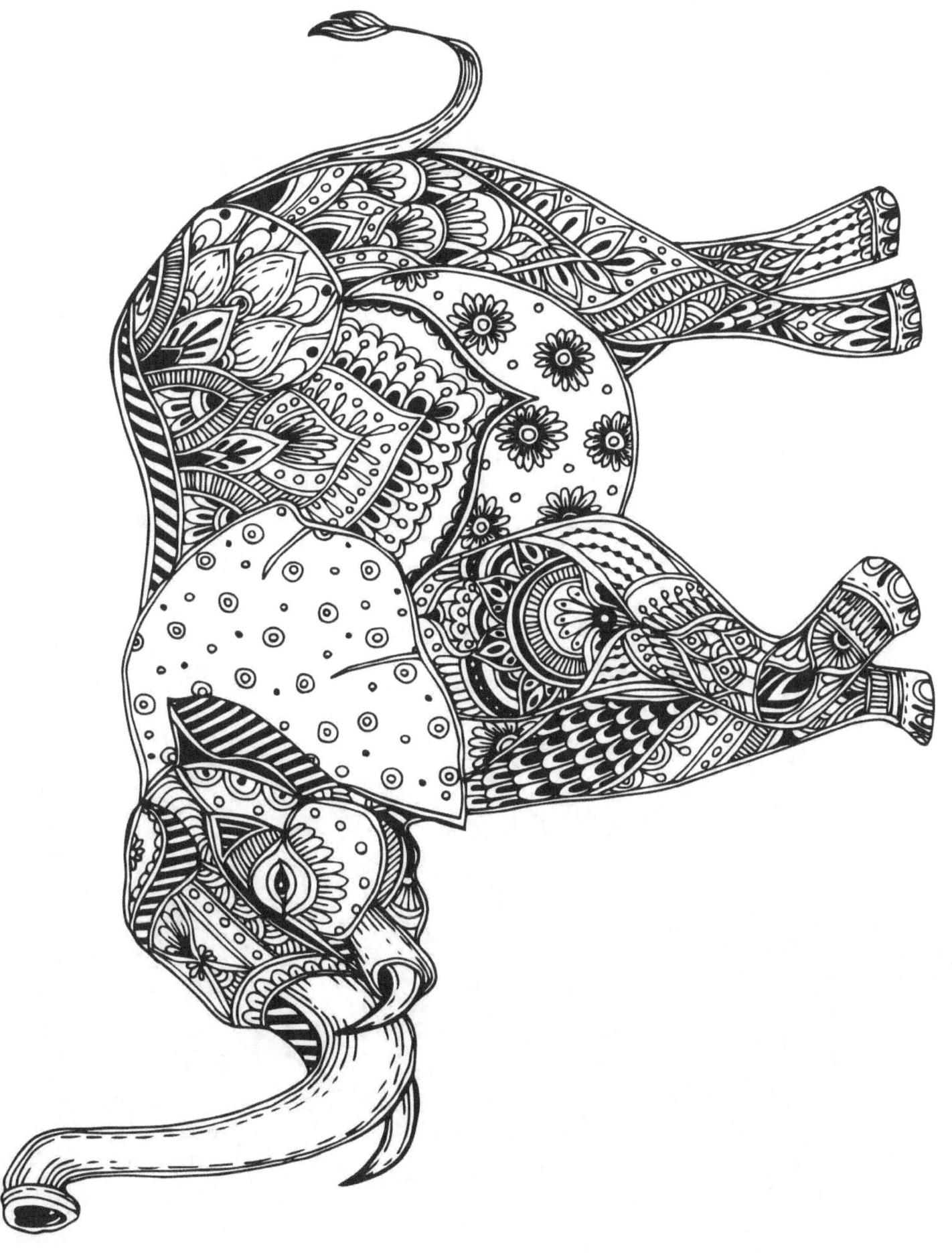

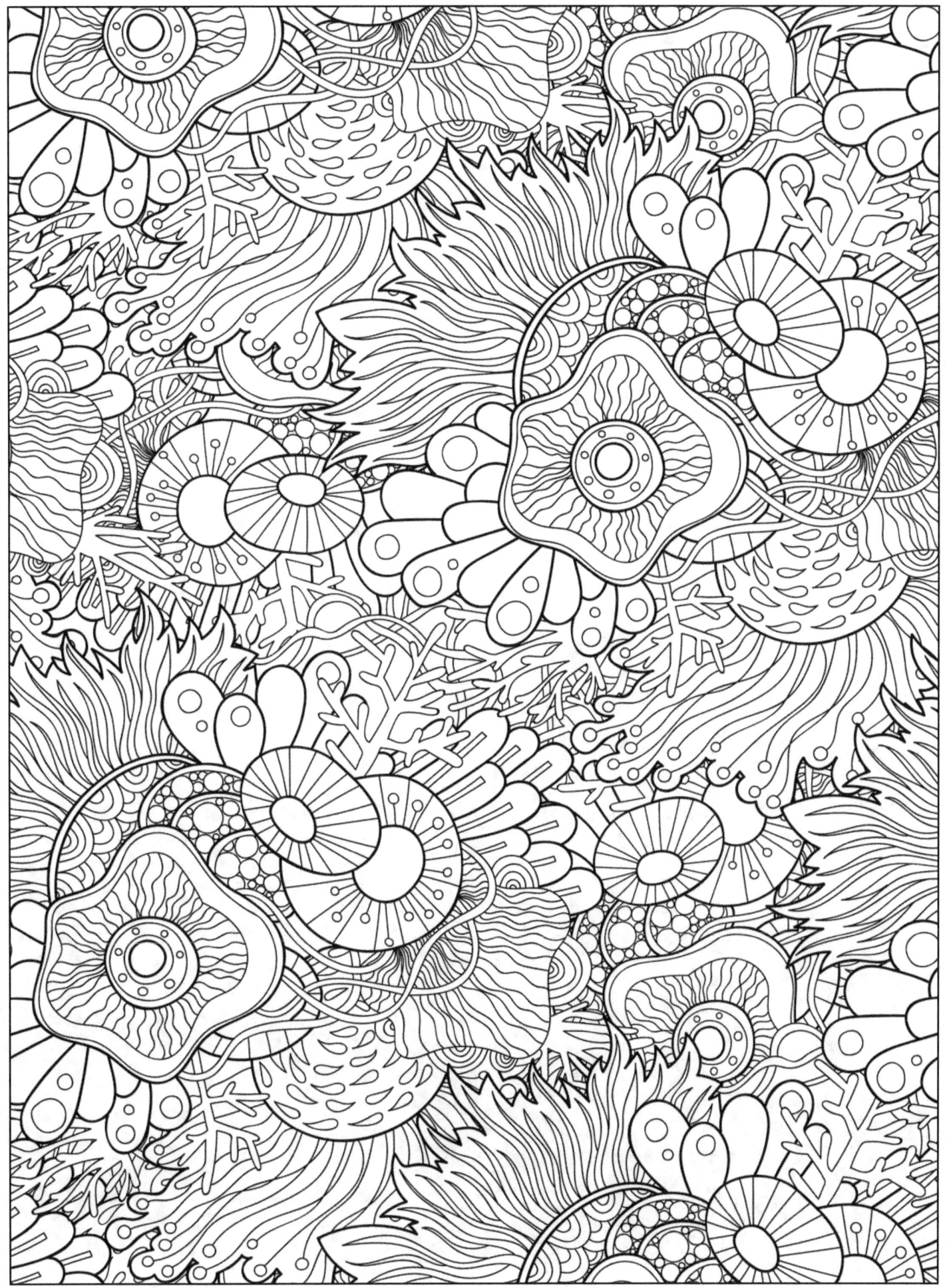

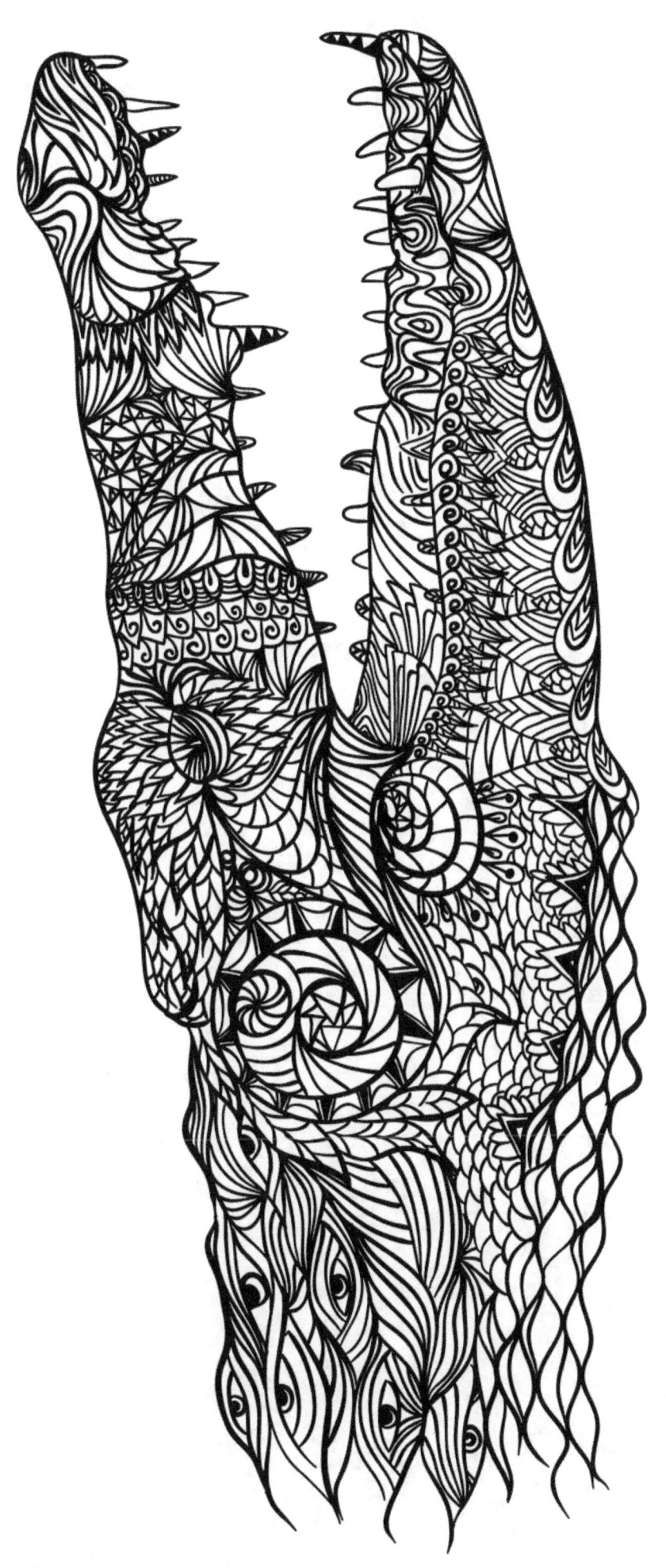

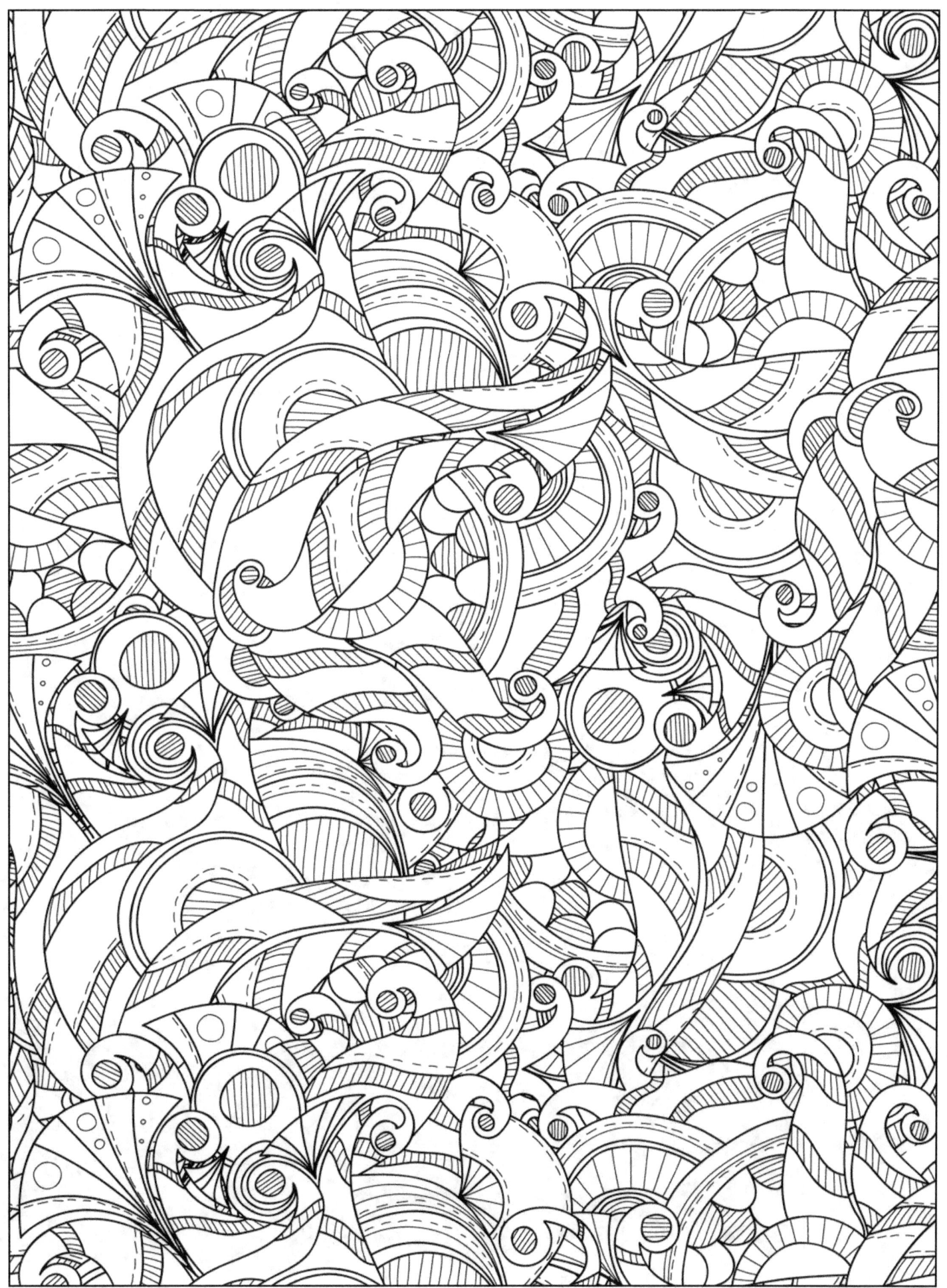

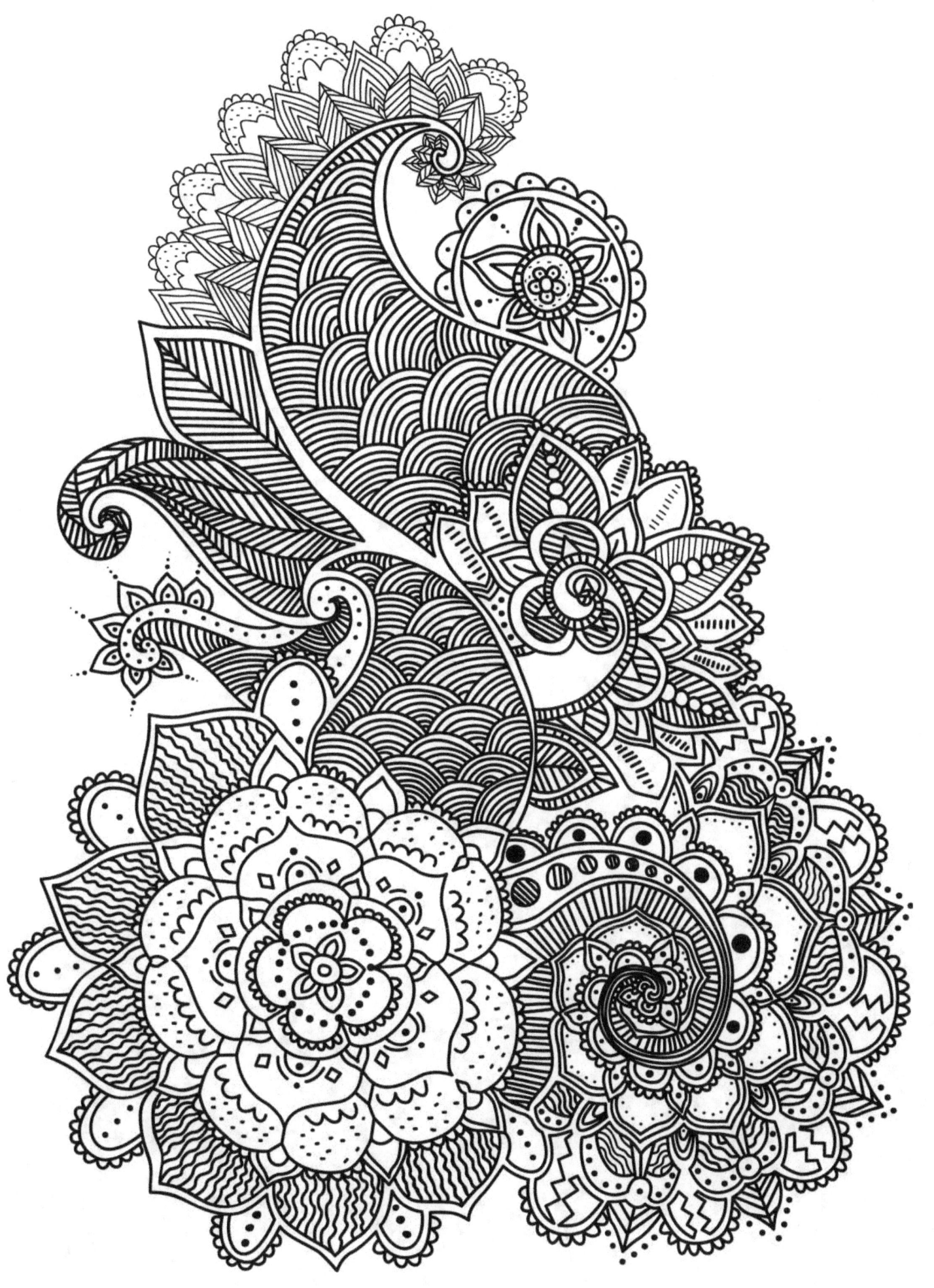

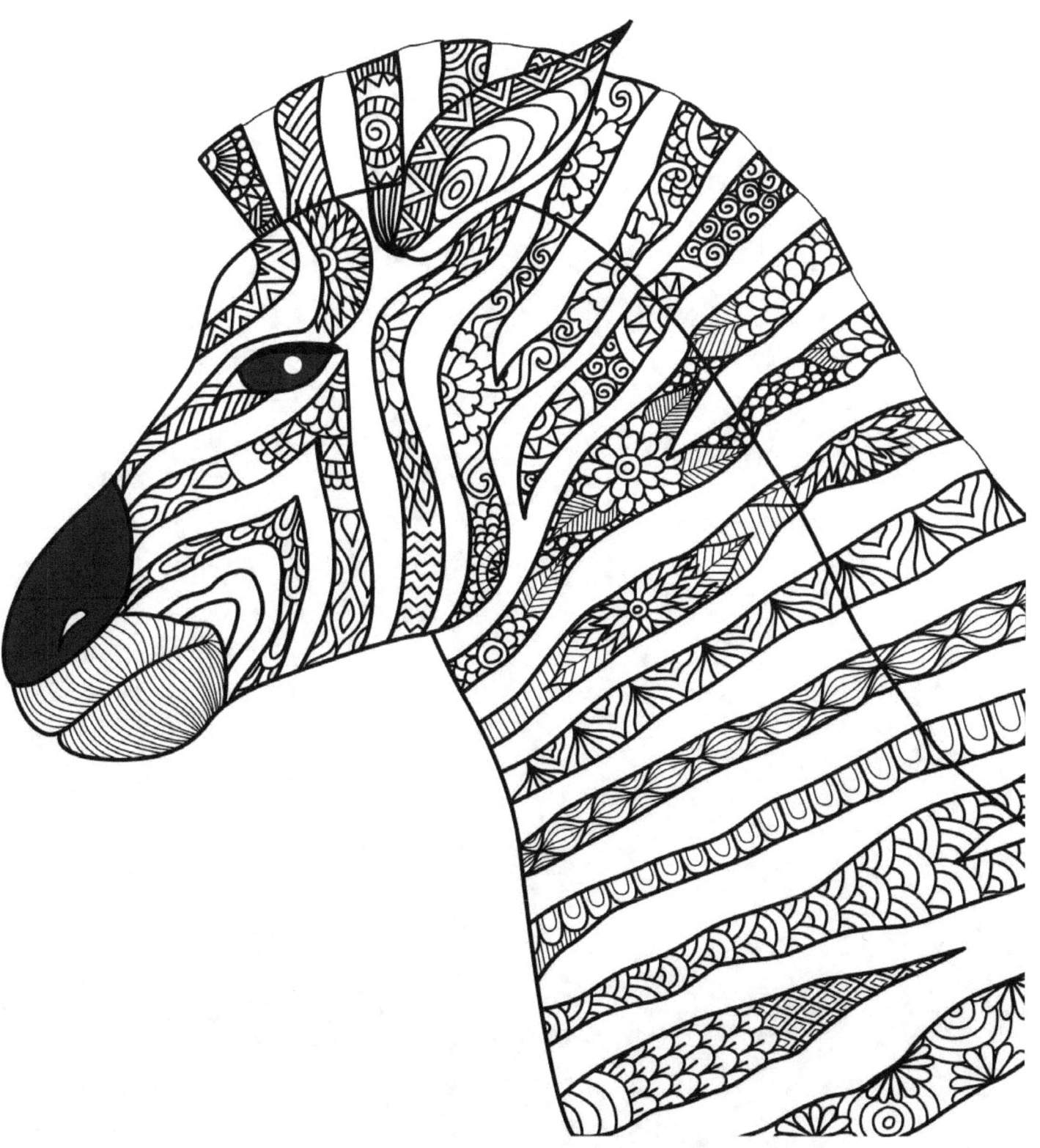

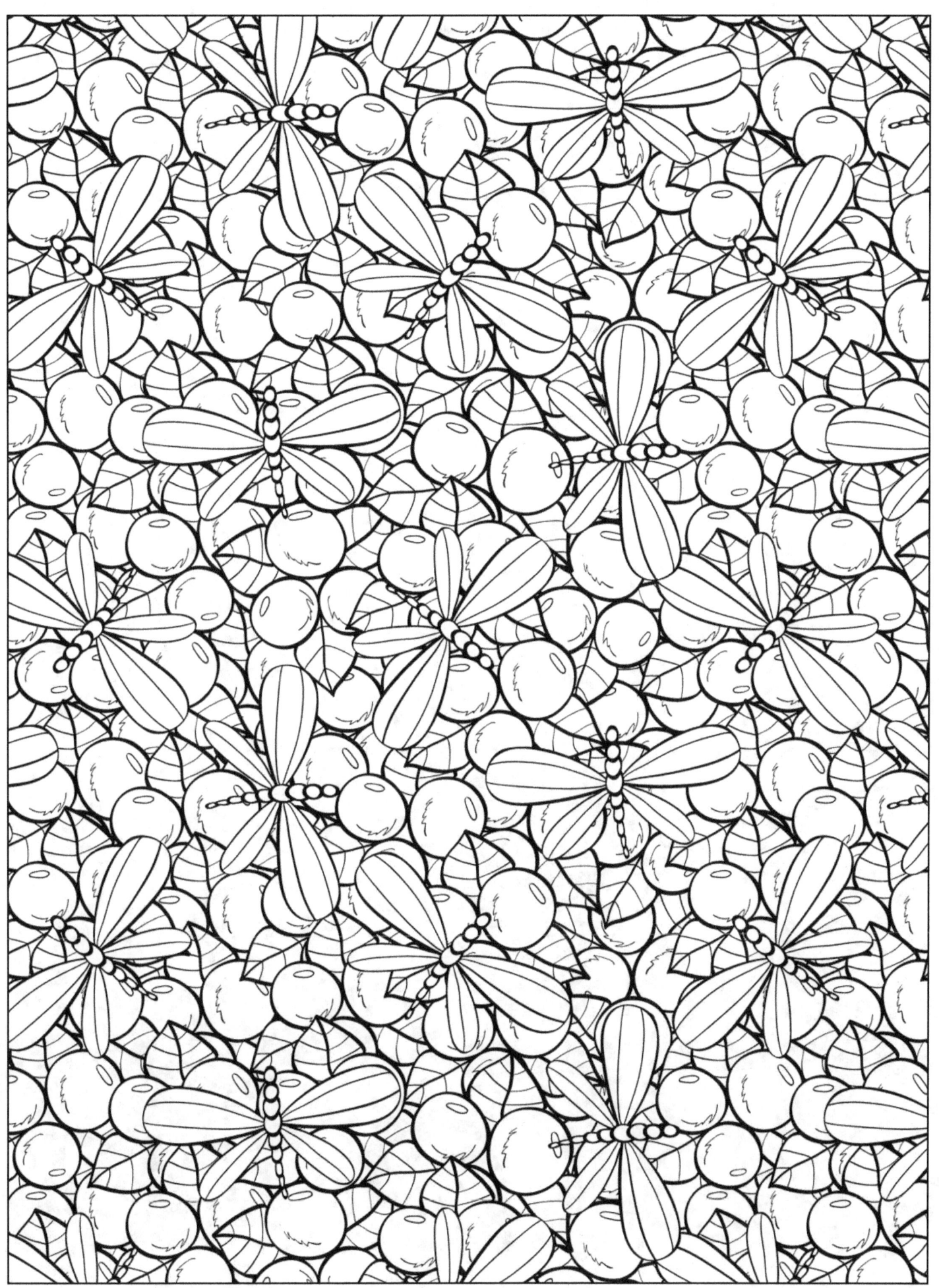

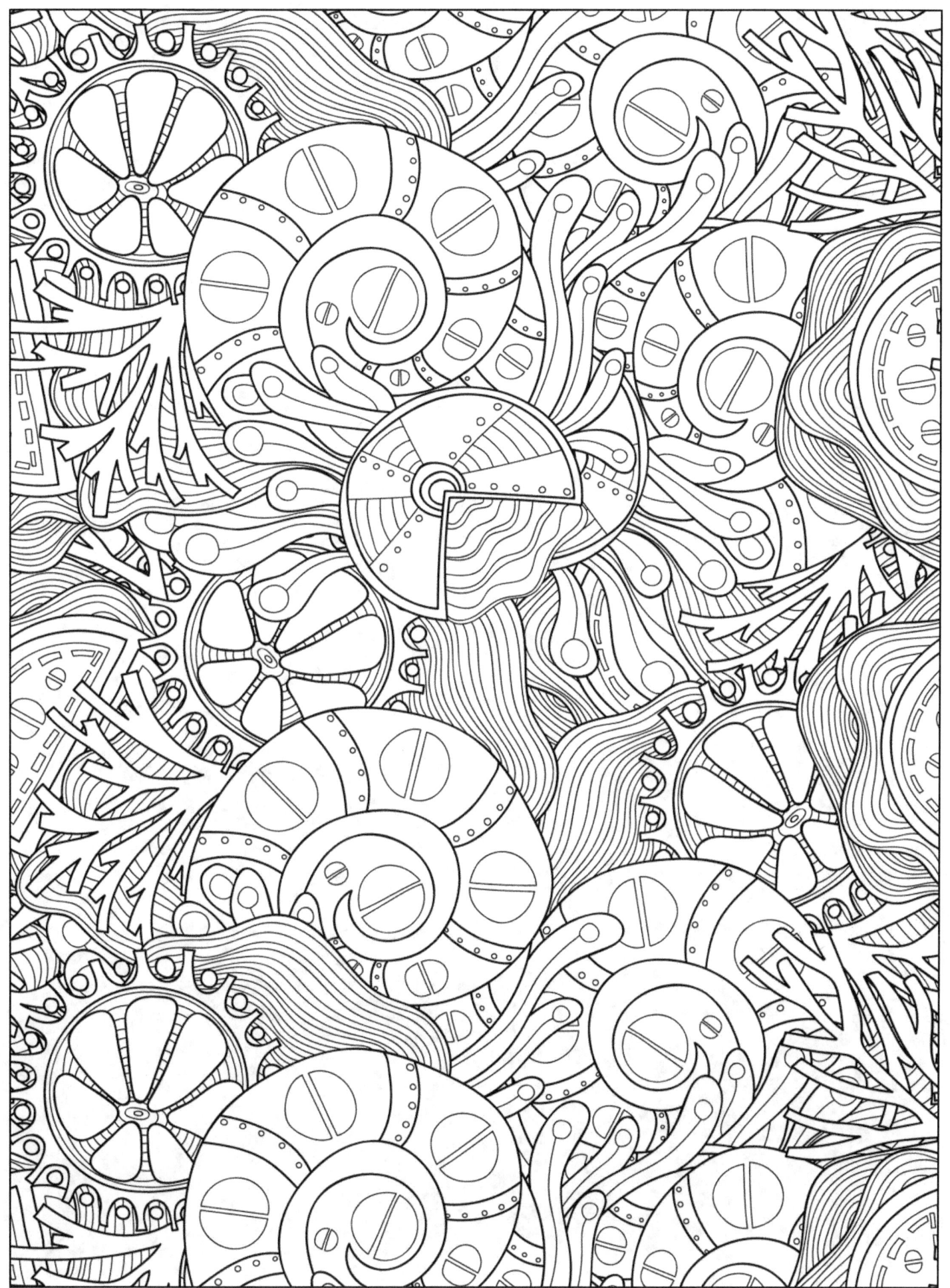

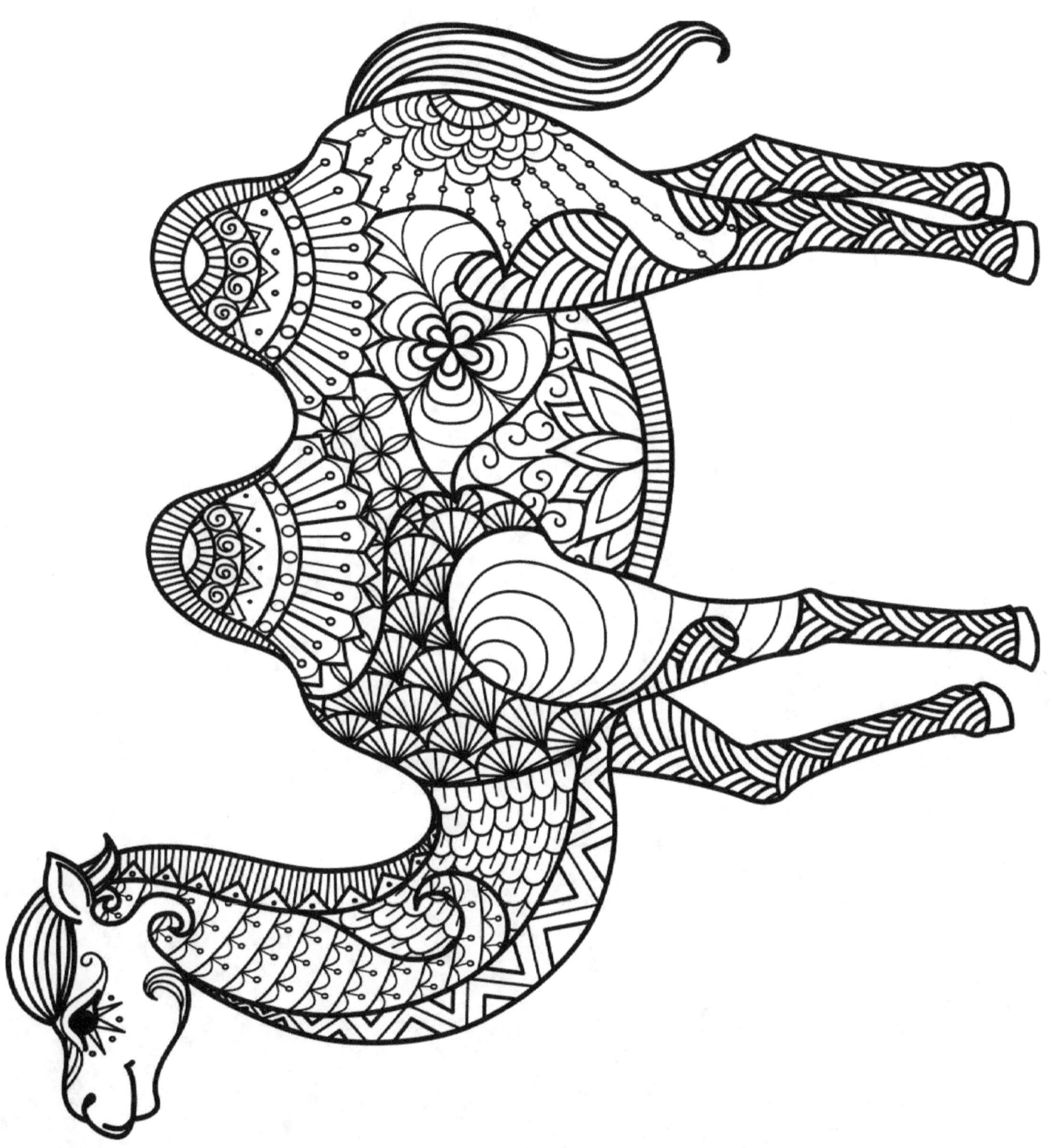

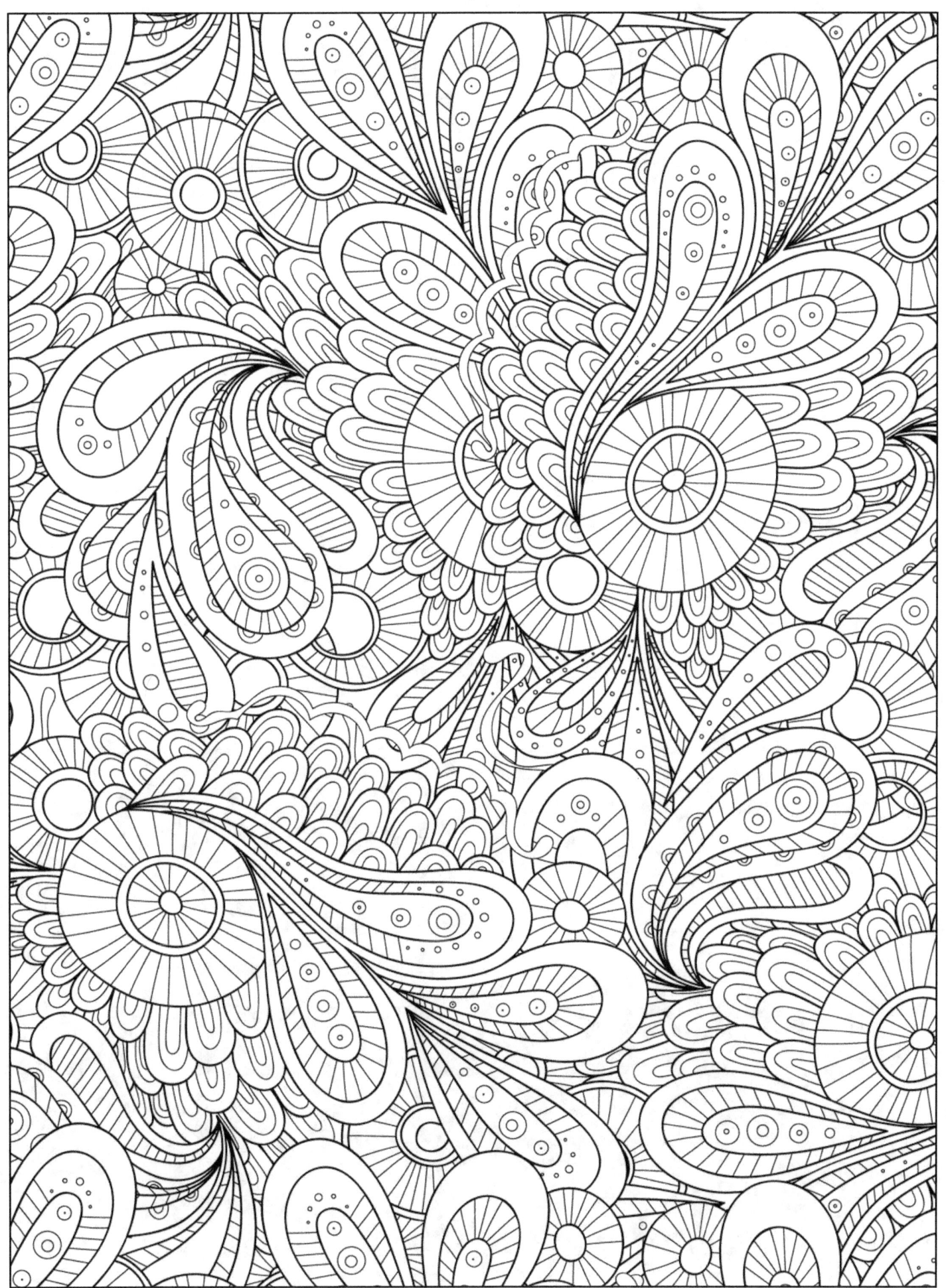

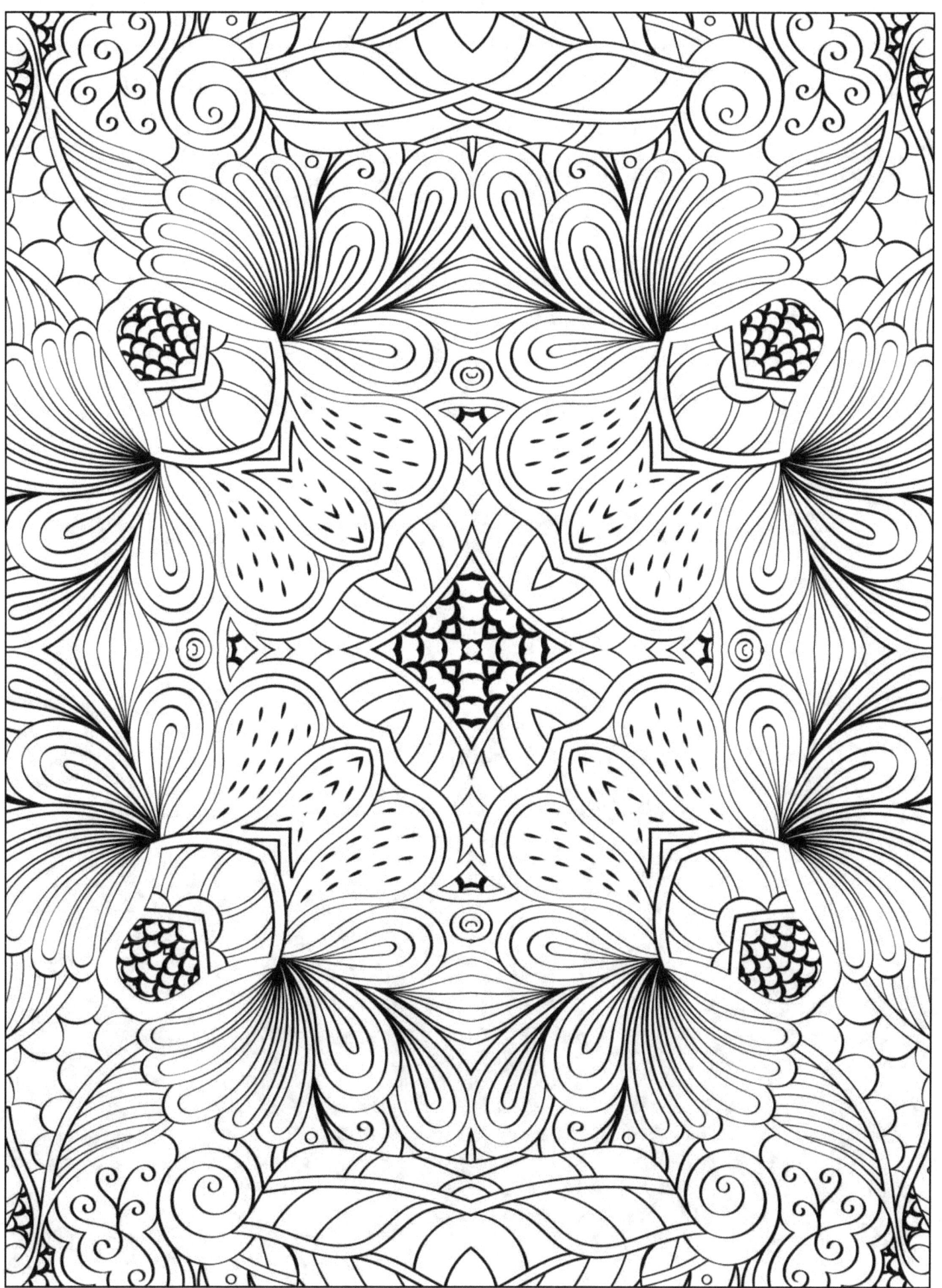

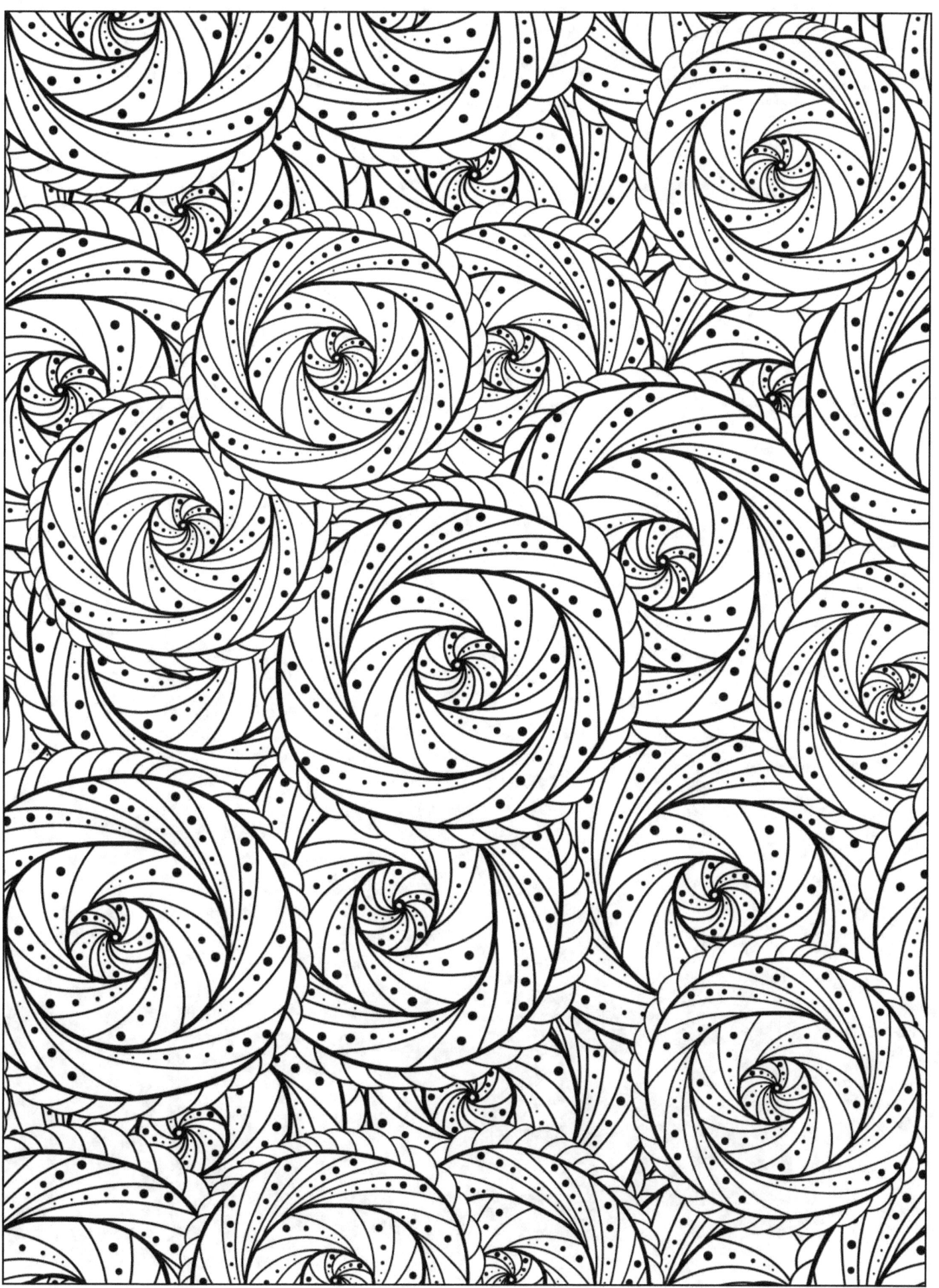

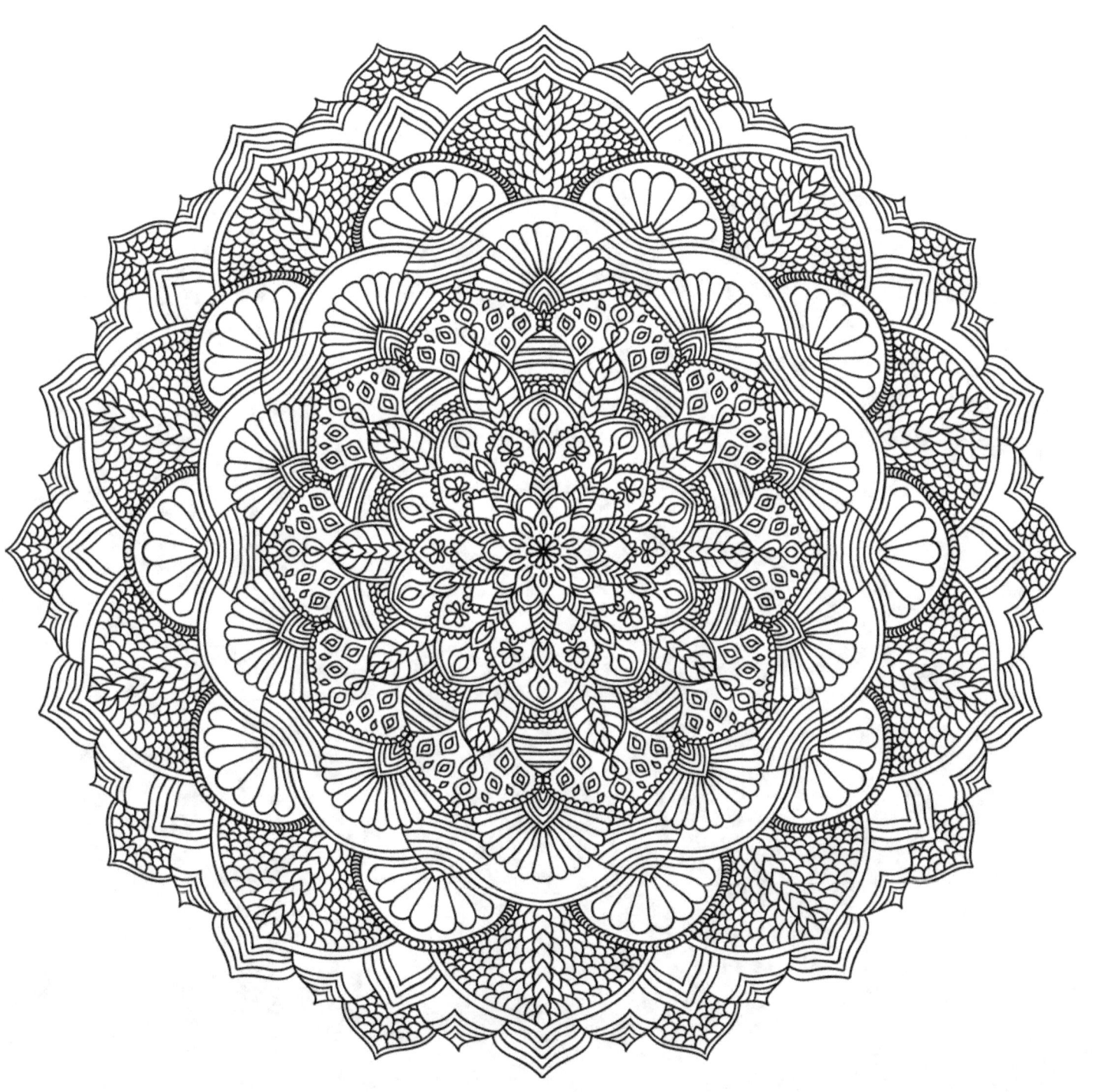

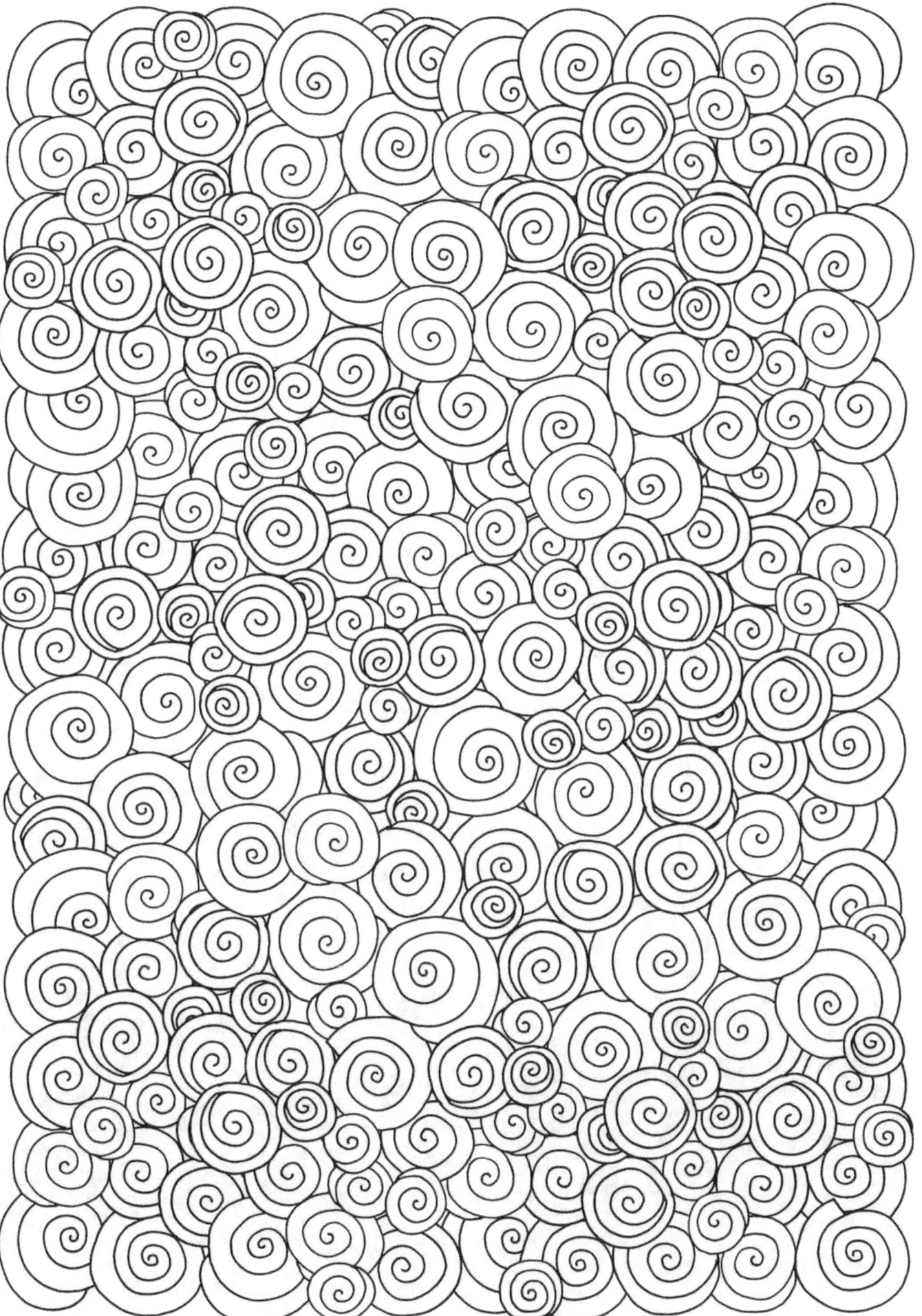

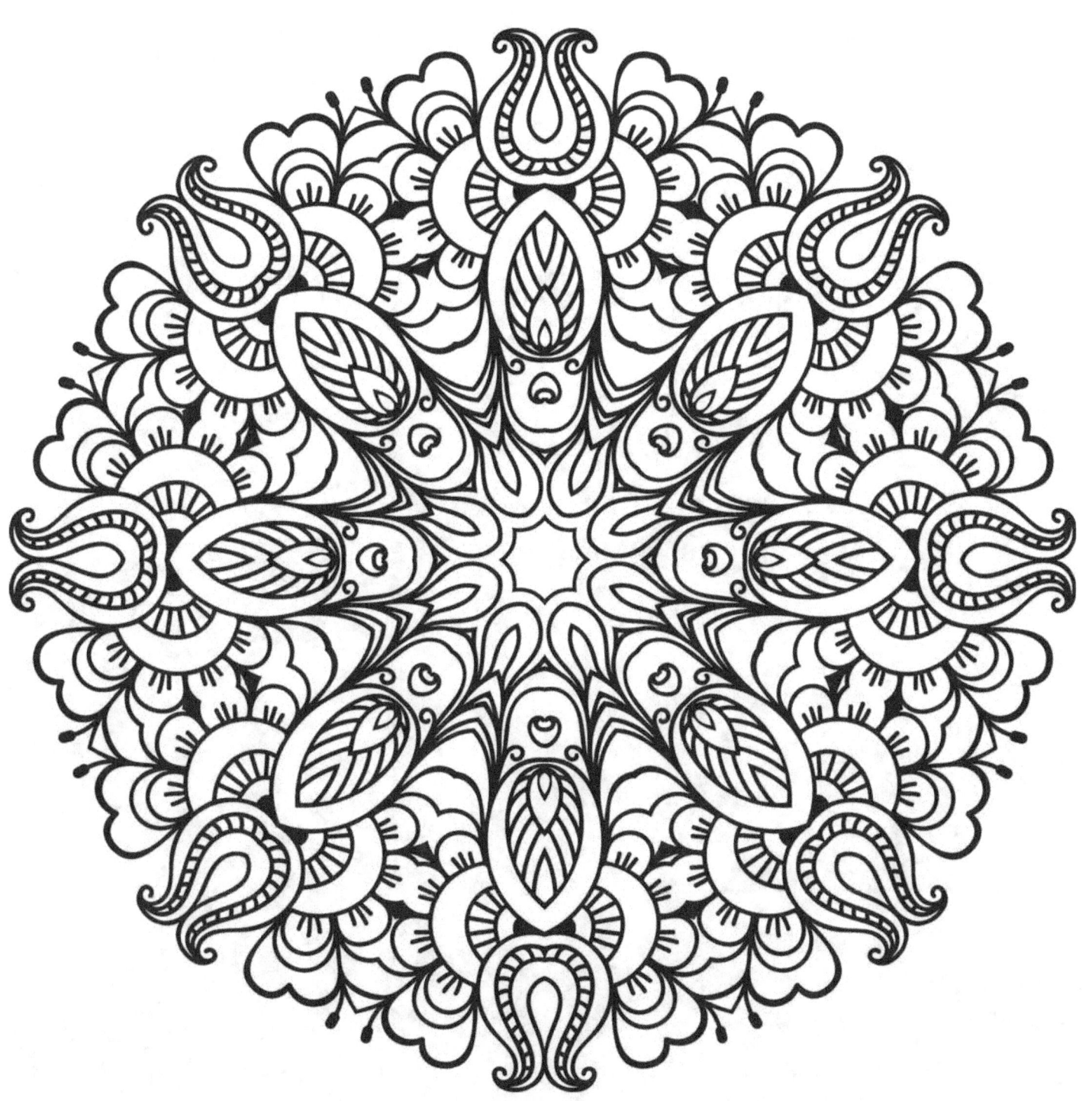

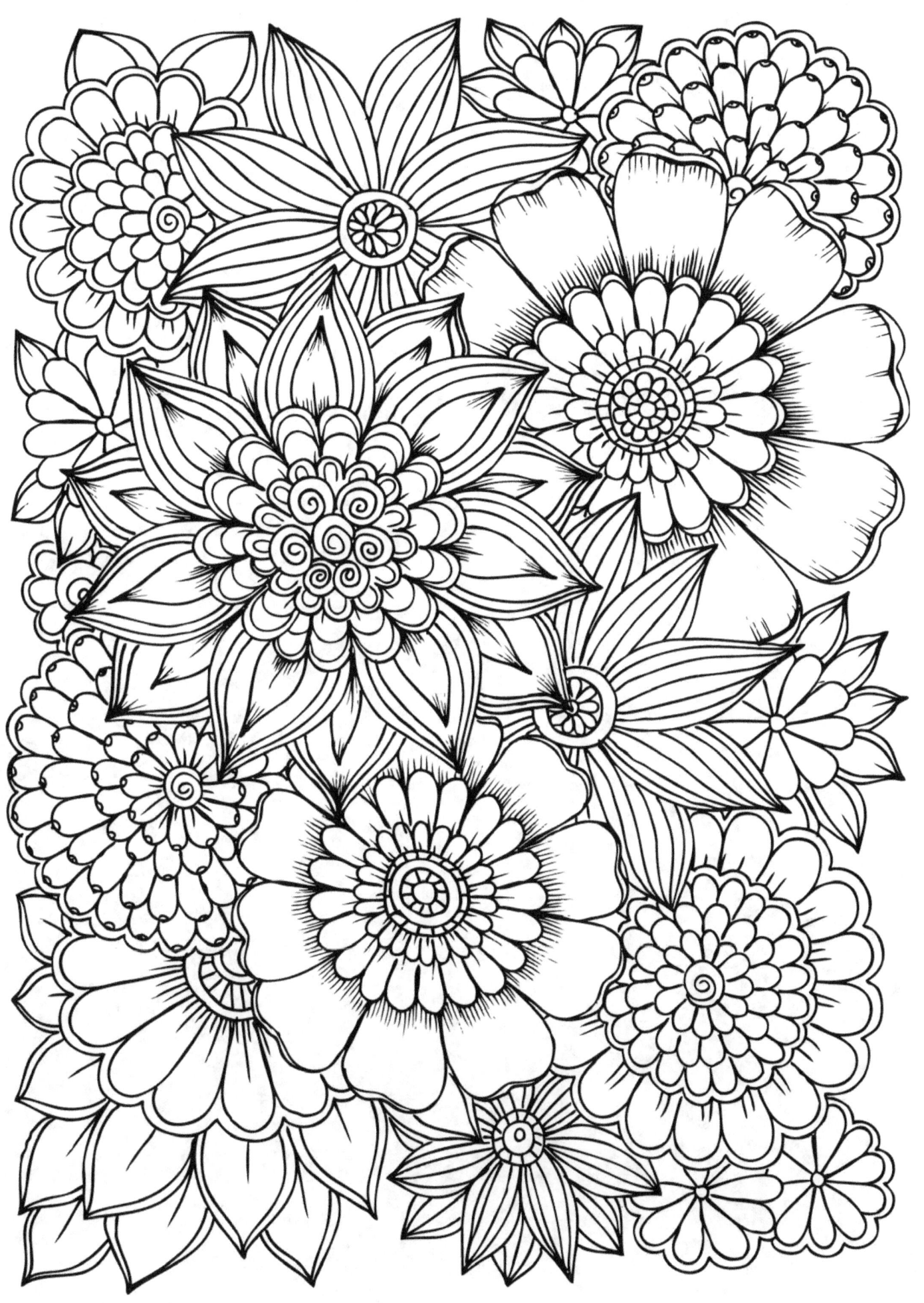

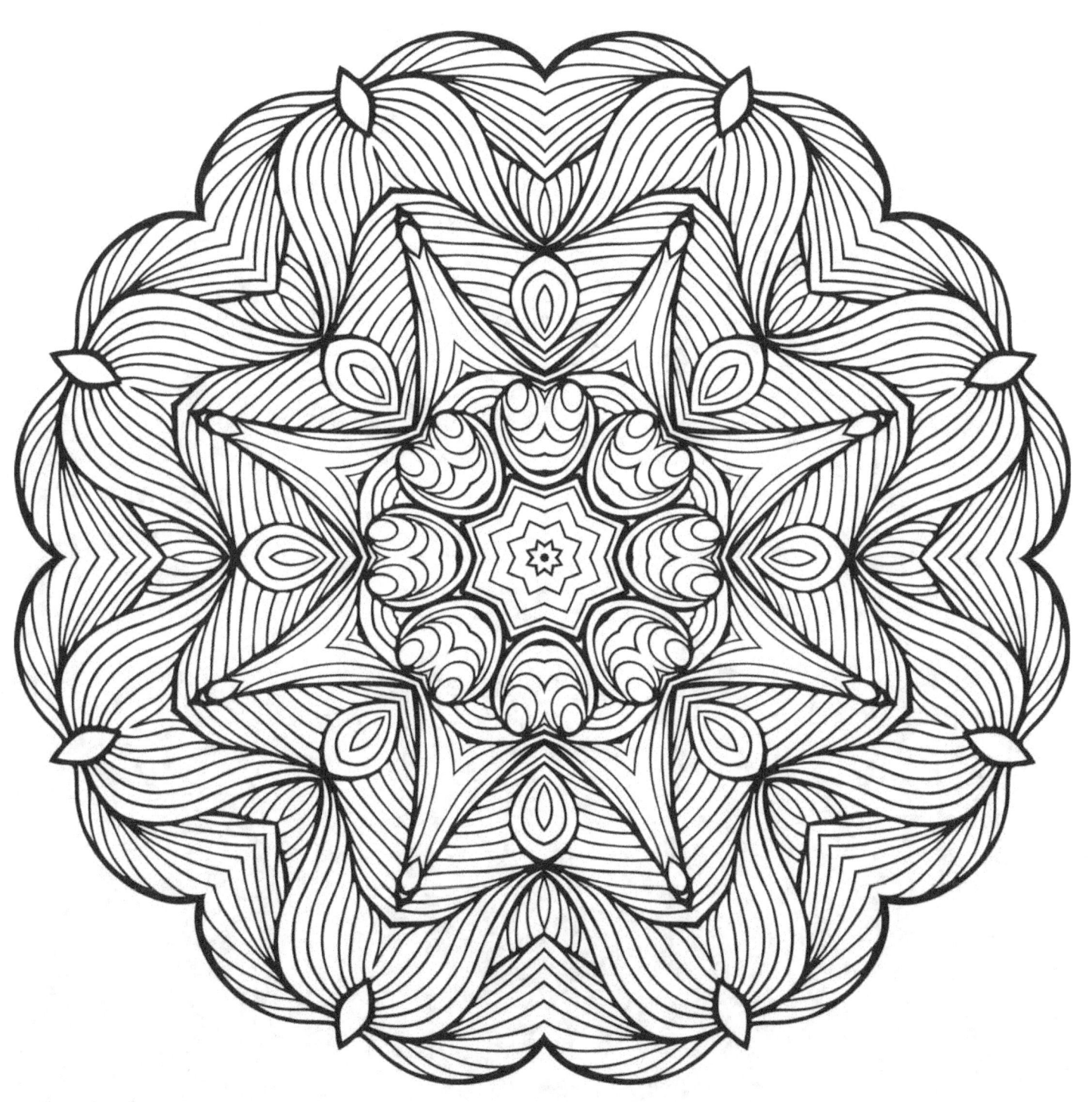

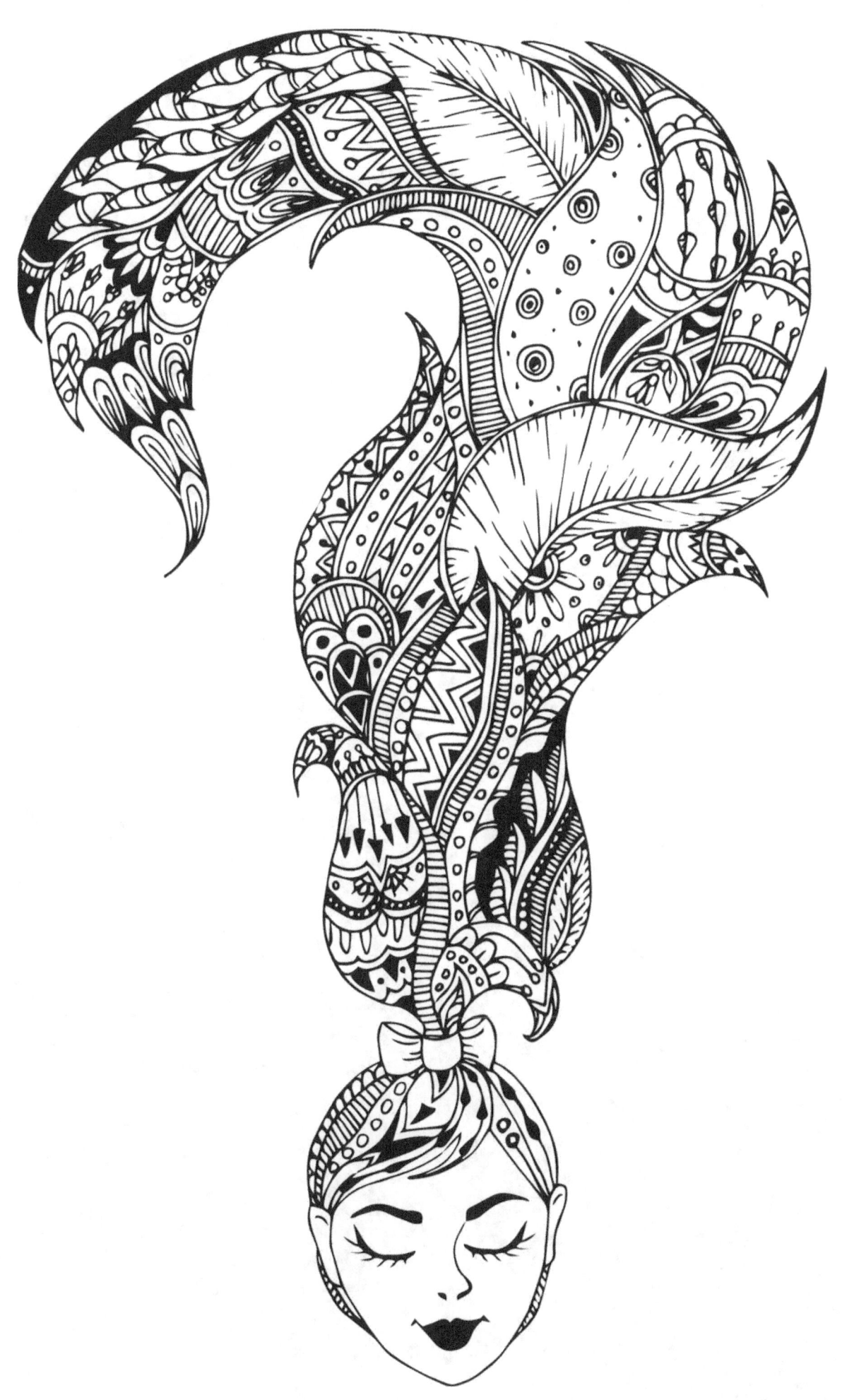

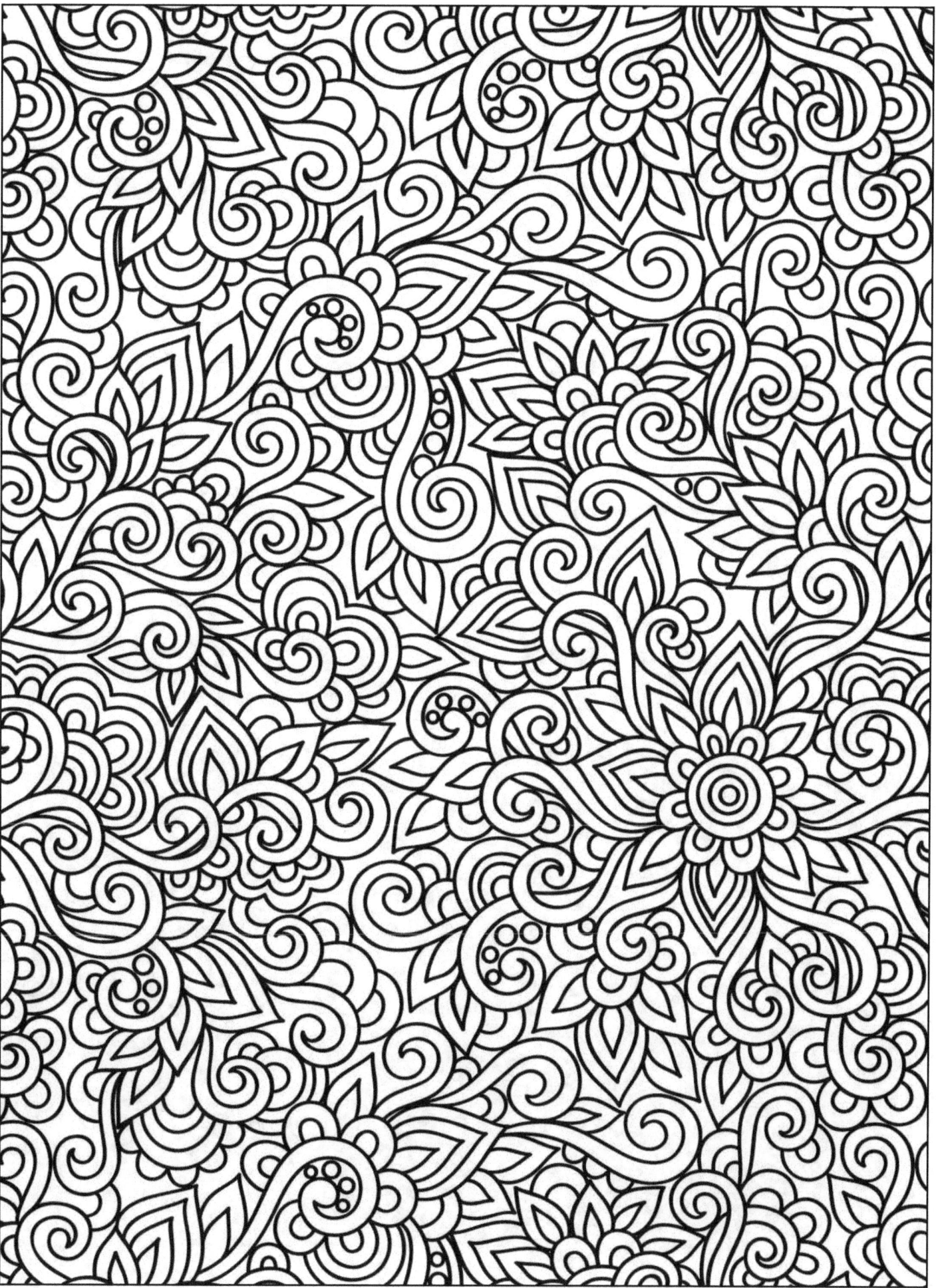

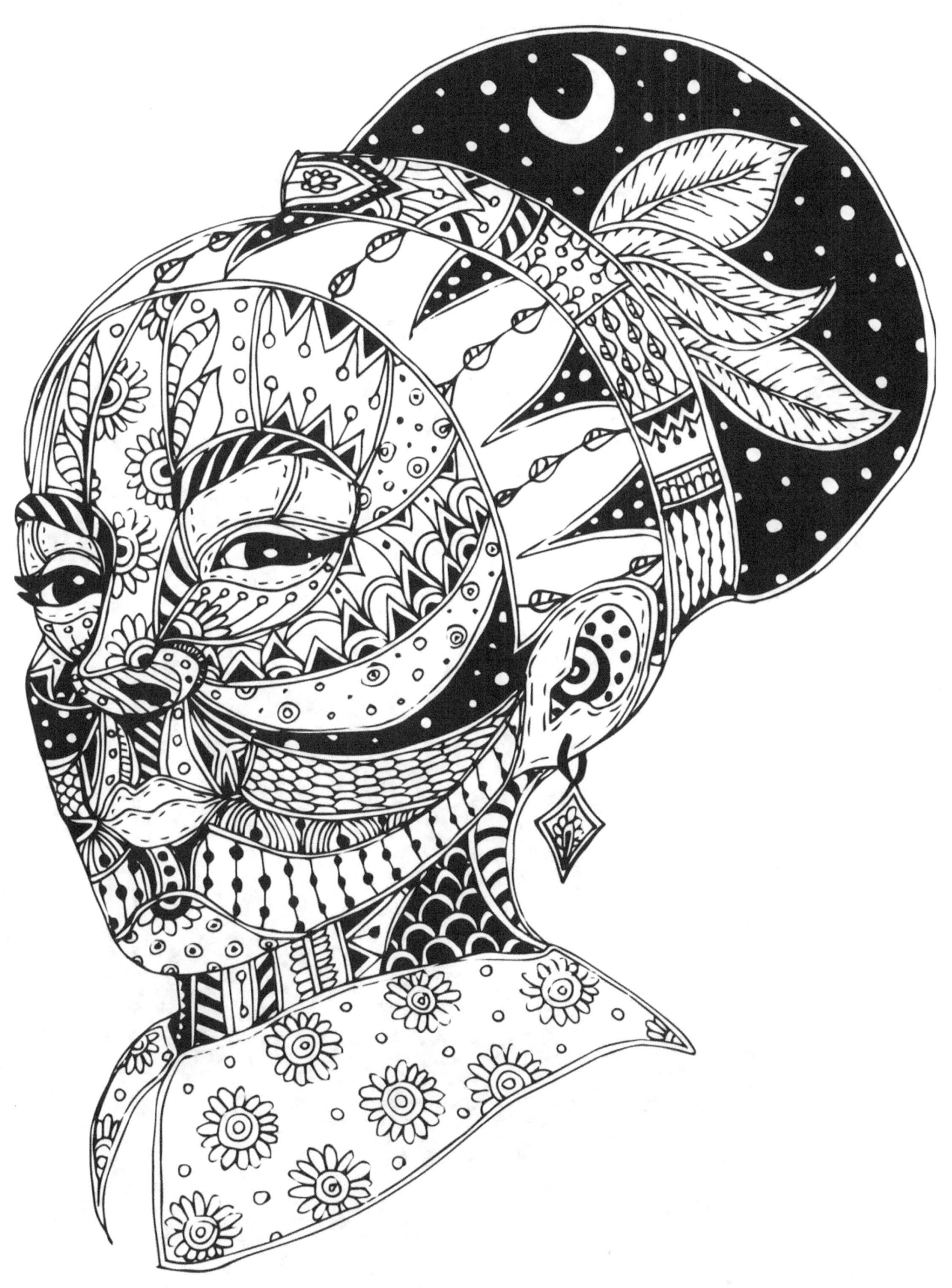

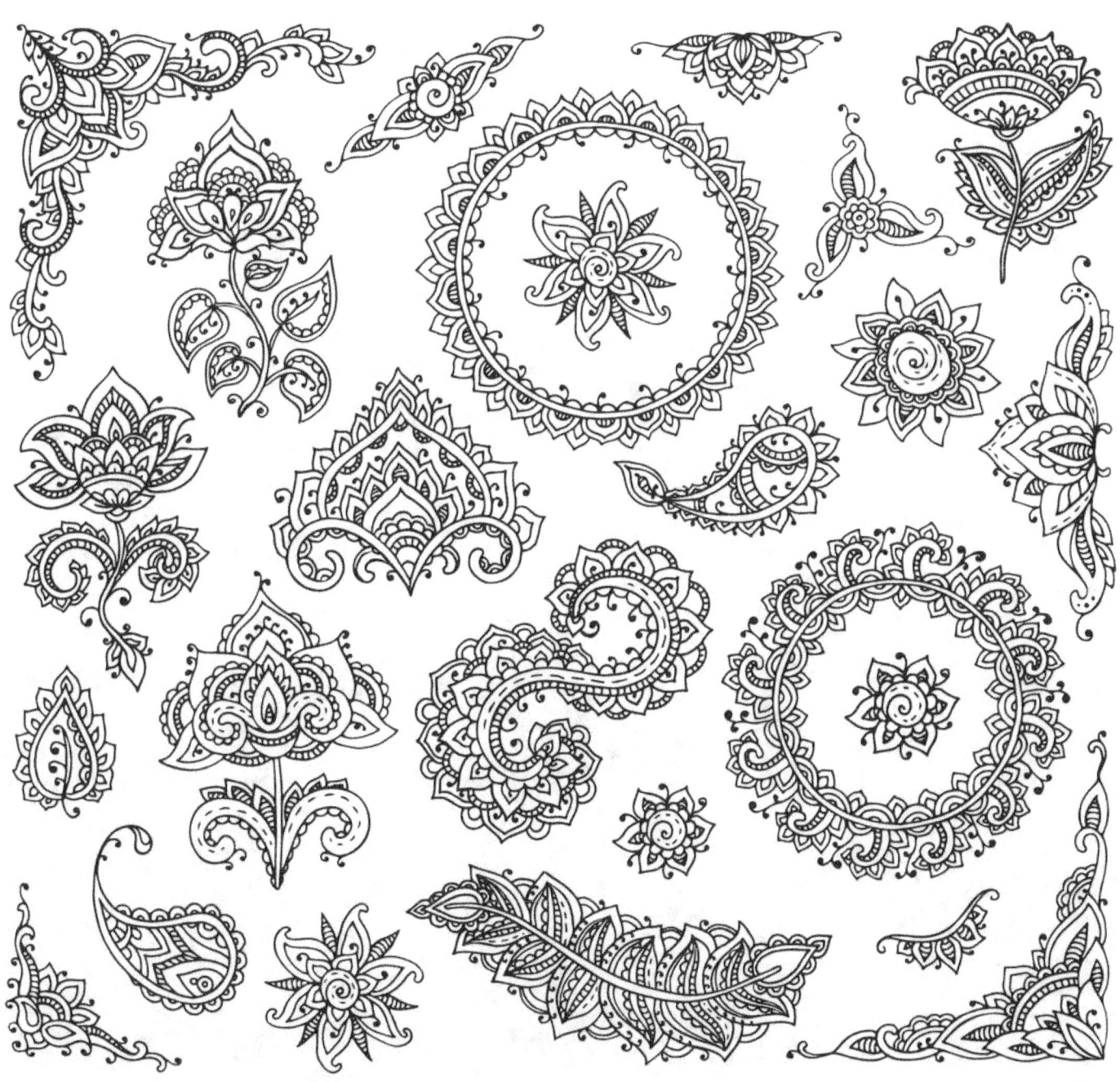

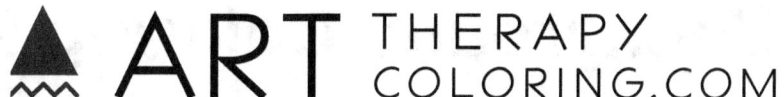

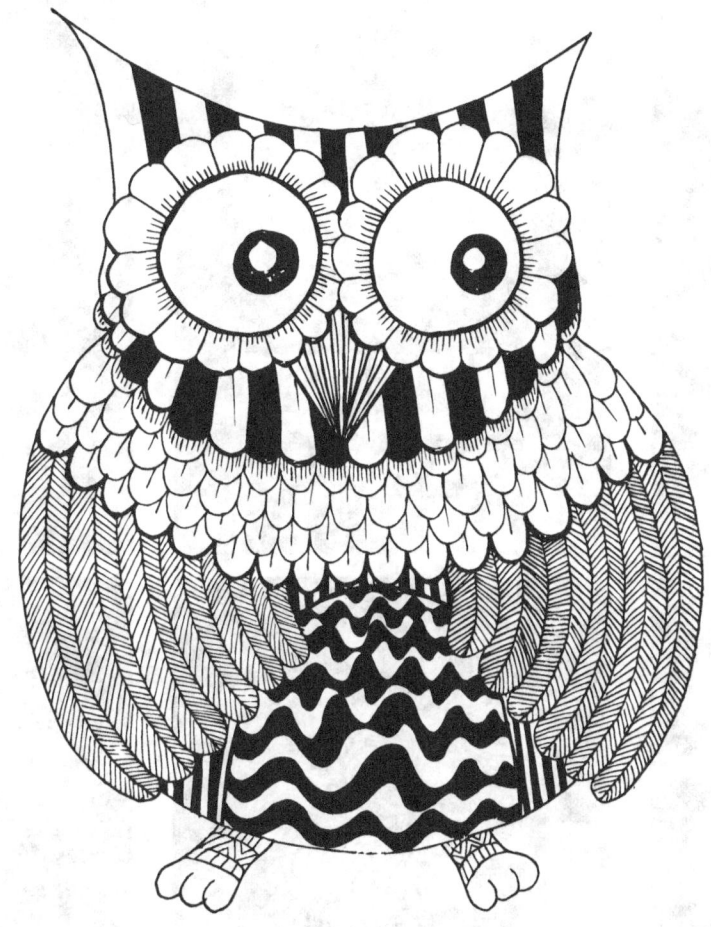

Visit our website at www.arttherapycoloring.com

Get a Free Printable Coloring Ebook!

We've created an exclusive offer for our customers to receive a free Adult Coloring Ebook.

Visit **www.arttherapycoloring.com/freebie** to claim your free coloring book with over 30 new designs that you can instantly print and color!

Over 100 Anti-Stress Adult Coloring Books

See our collection of over 100 anti-stress coloring books for adults and teens on the following pages available at Amazon.com and other online retailers.

Black Background Coloring Books

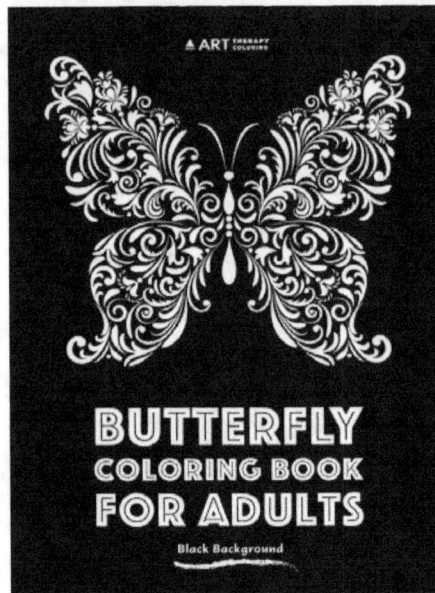

BUTTERFLY
COLORING BOOK
FOR ADULTS
Black Background

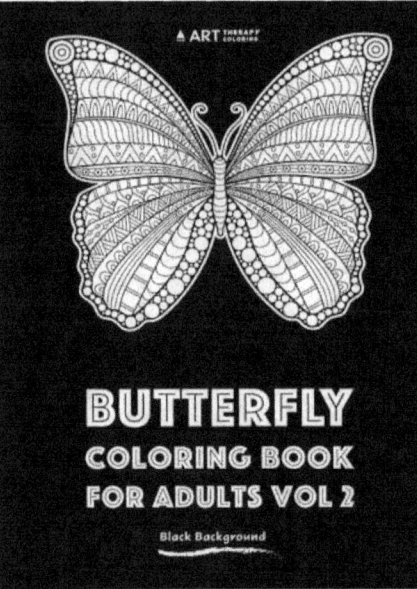

BUTTERFLY
COLORING BOOK
FOR ADULTS VOL 2
Black Background

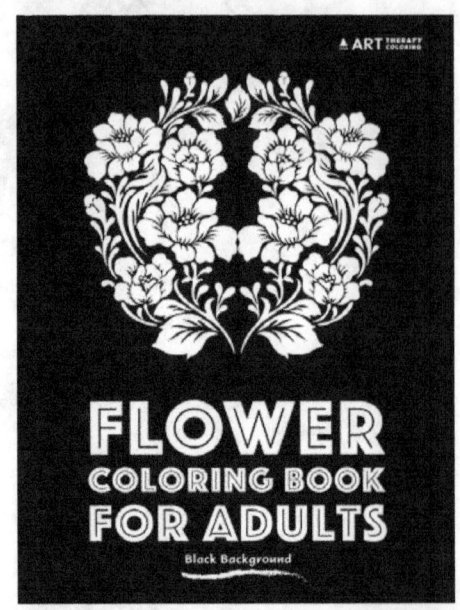

FLOWER
COLORING BOOK
FOR ADULTS
Black Background

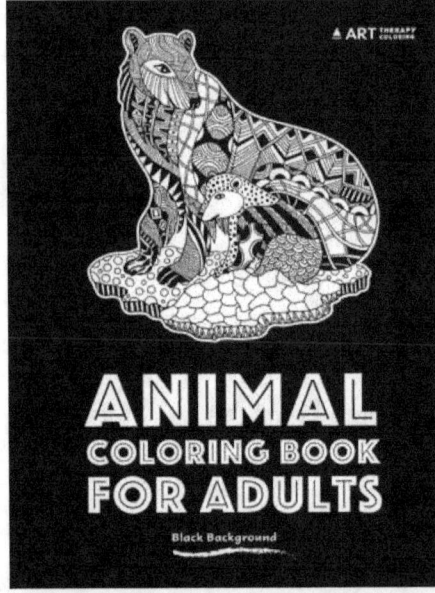

ANIMAL
COLORING BOOK
FOR ADULTS
Black Background

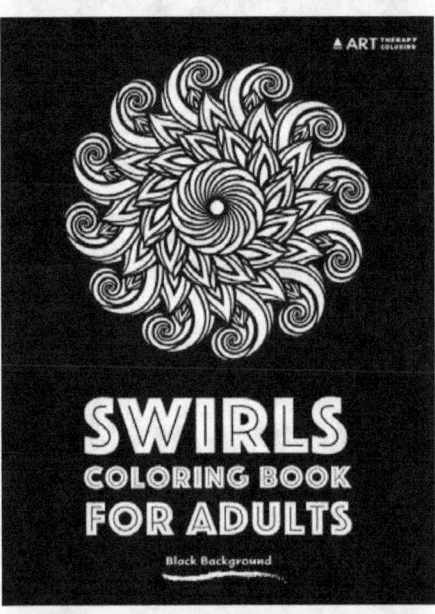

SWIRLS
COLORING BOOK
FOR ADULTS
Black Background

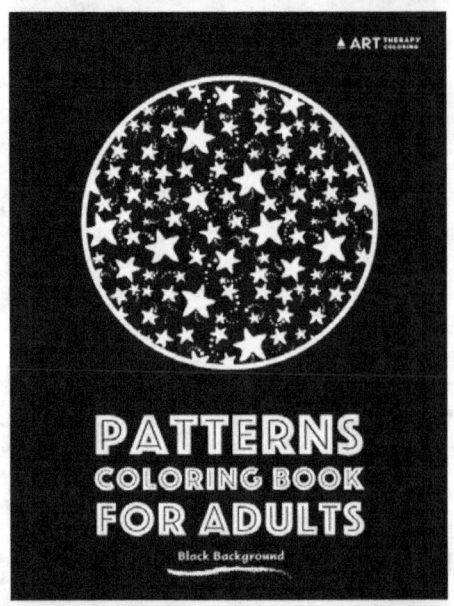

PATTERNS
COLORING BOOK
FOR ADULTS
Black Background

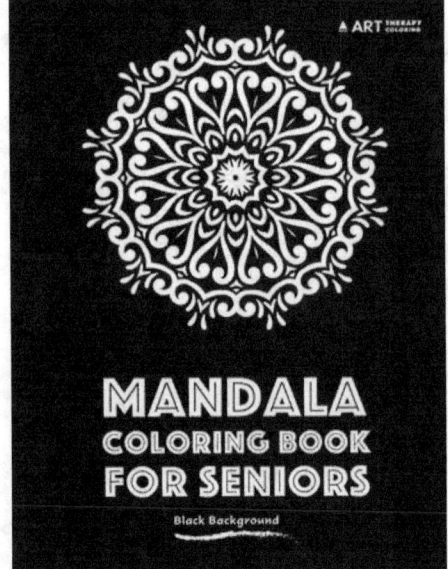

MANDALA
COLORING BOOK
FOR SENIORS
Black Background

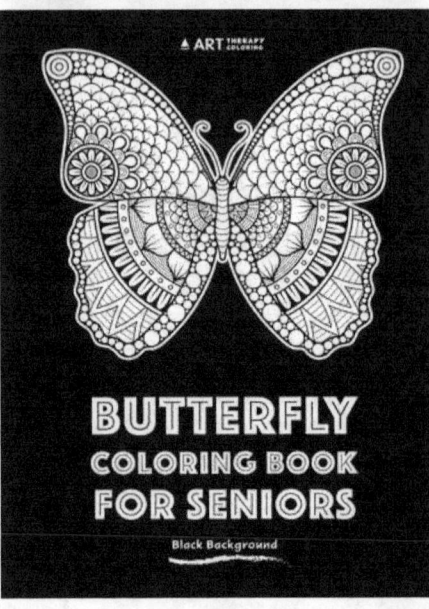

BUTTERFLY
COLORING BOOK
FOR SENIORS
Black Background

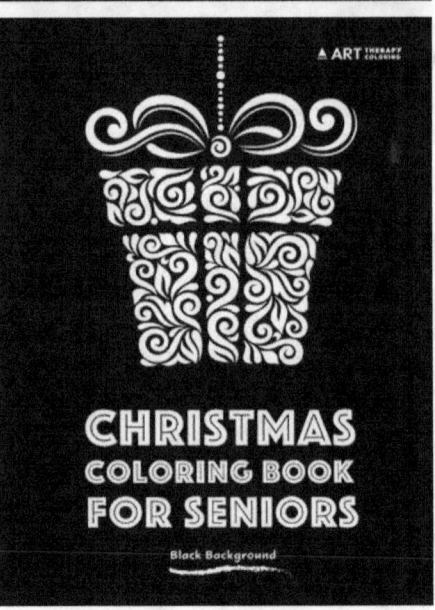

CHRISTMAS
COLORING BOOK
FOR SENIORS
Black Background

Black Background Coloring Books

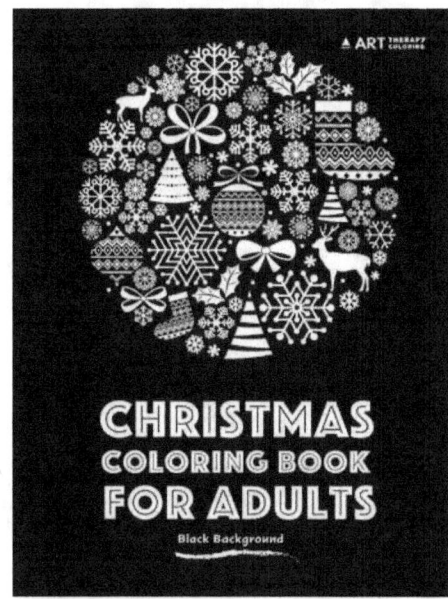

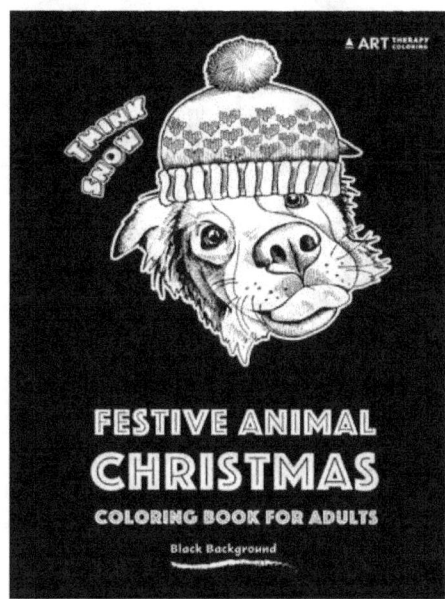

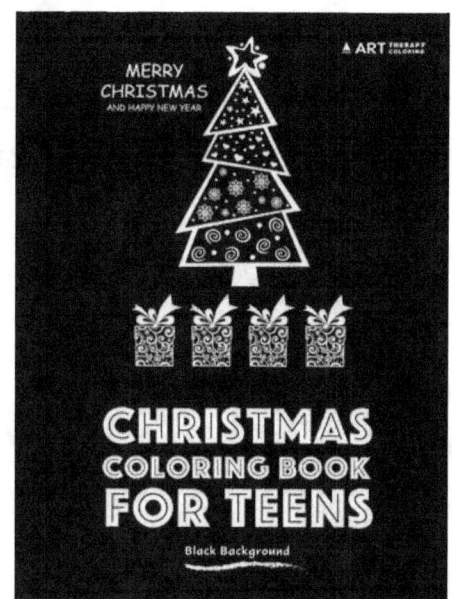

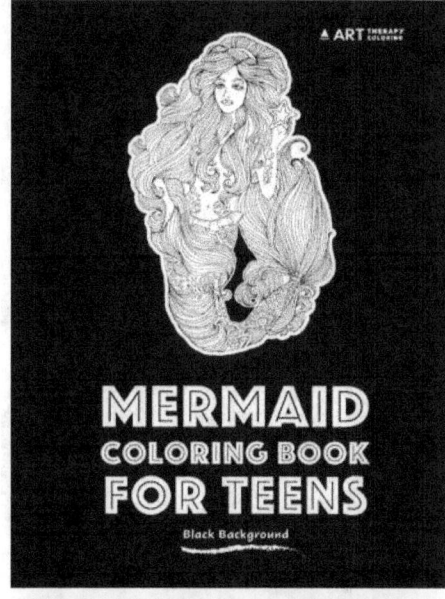

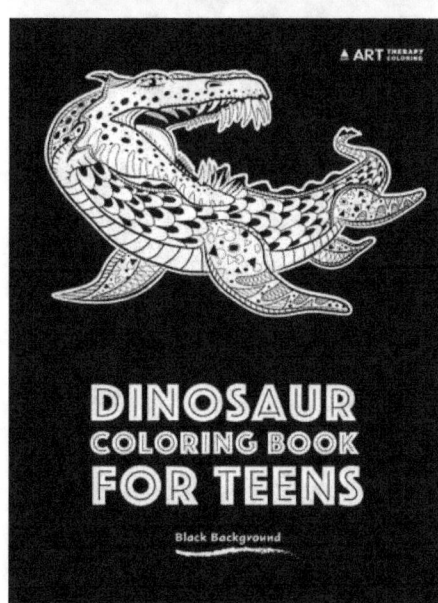

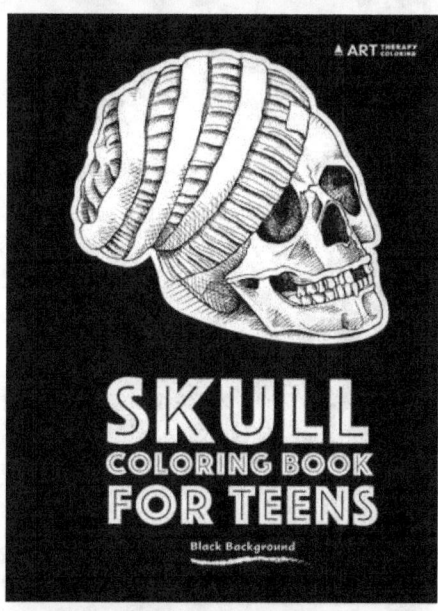

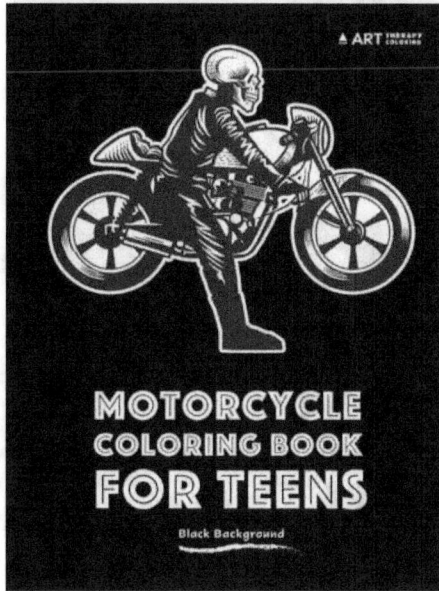

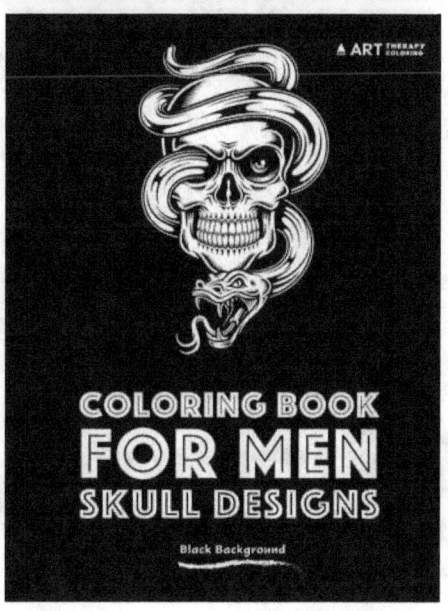

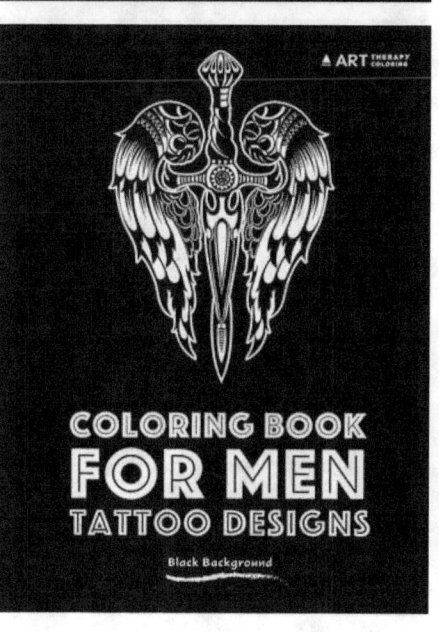

www.arttherapycoloring.com

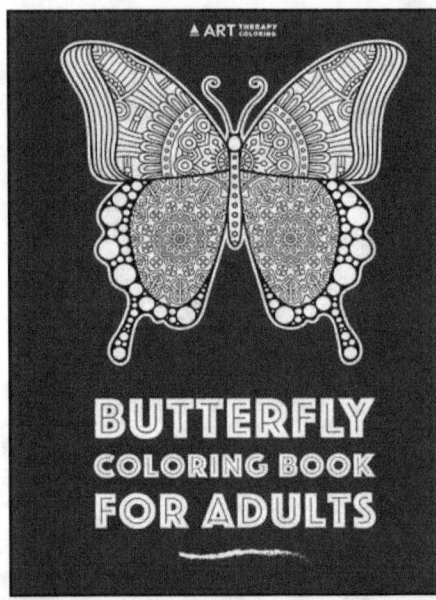

BUTTERFLY
COLORING BOOK
FOR ADULTS

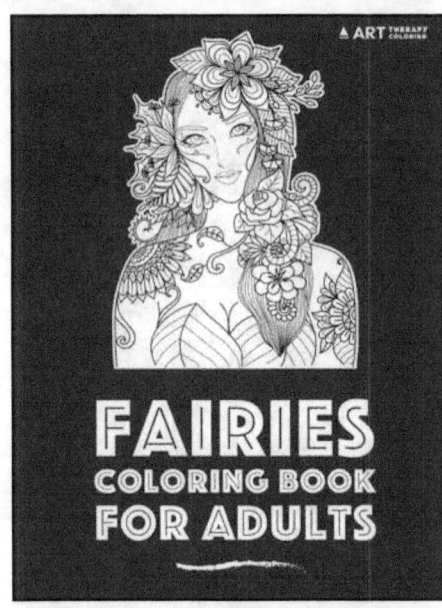

FAIRIES
COLORING BOOK
FOR ADULTS

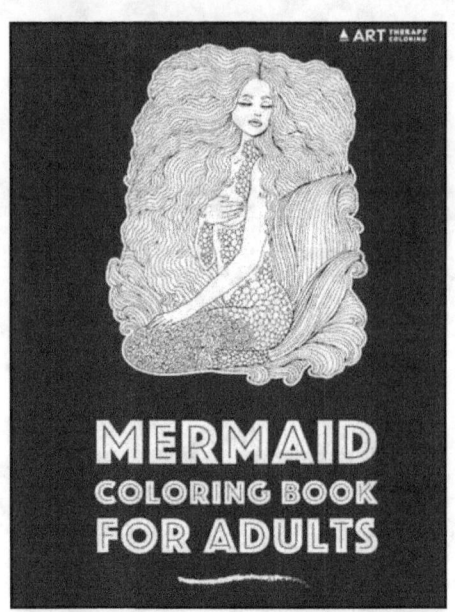

MERMAID
COLORING BOOK
FOR ADULTS

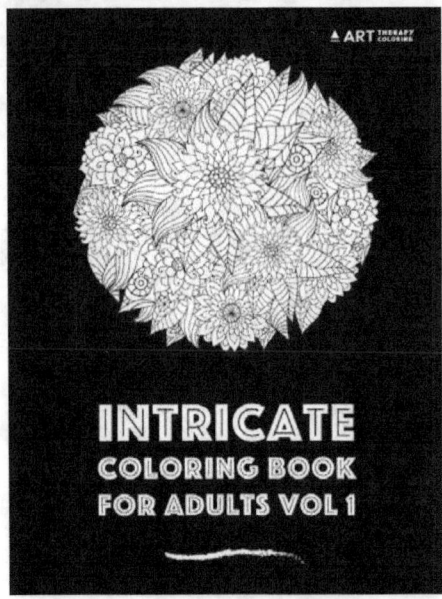

INTRICATE
COLORING BOOK
FOR ADULTS VOL 1

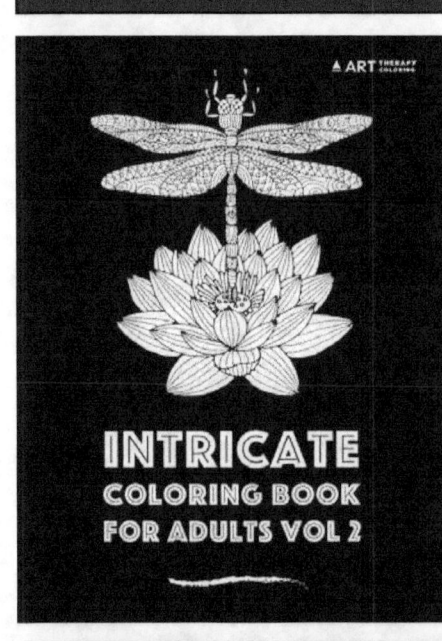

INTRICATE
COLORING BOOK
FOR ADULTS VOL 2

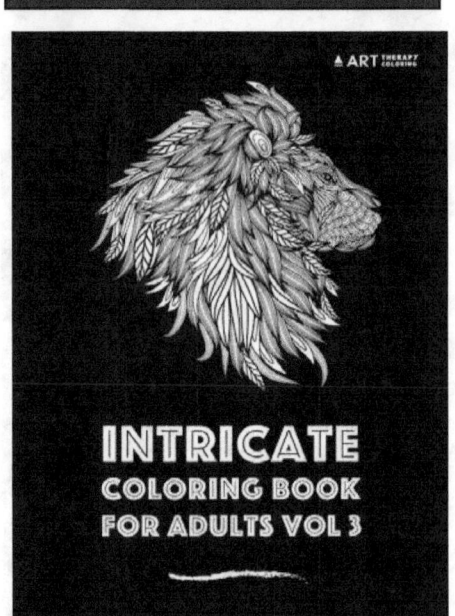

INTRICATE
COLORING BOOK
FOR ADULTS VOL 3

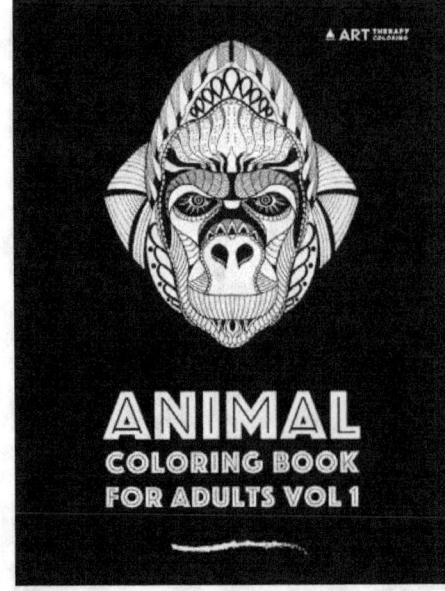

ANIMAL
COLORING BOOK
FOR ADULTS VOL 1

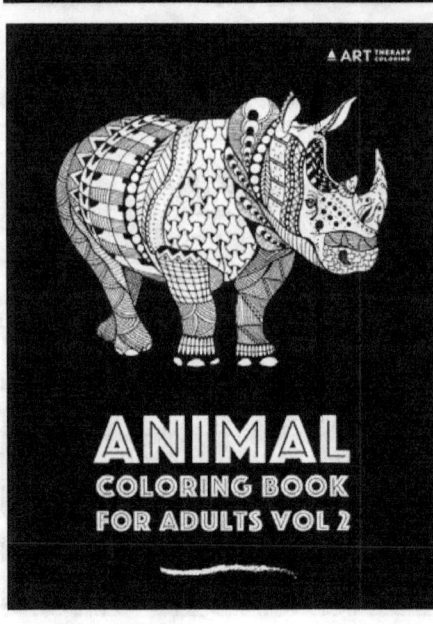

ANIMAL
COLORING BOOK
FOR ADULTS VOL 2

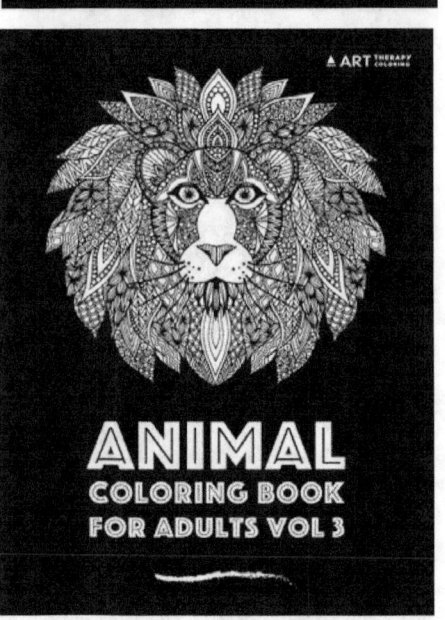

ANIMAL
COLORING BOOK
FOR ADULTS VOL 3

Art Therapy Coloring Books For Men

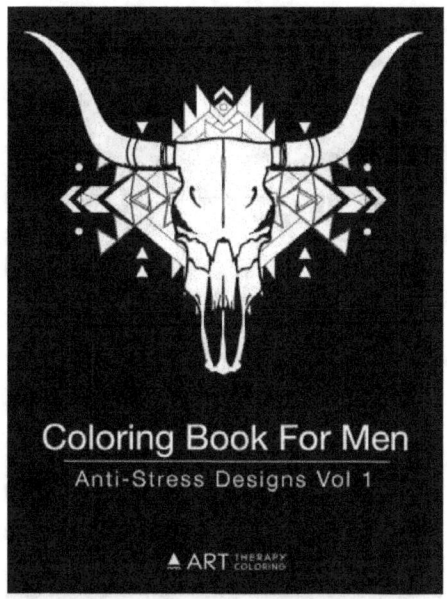

Coloring Book For Men
Anti-Stress Designs Vol 1

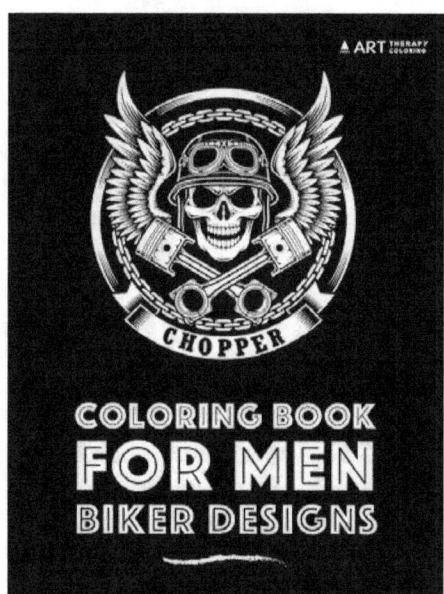

CHOPPER
COLORING BOOK
FOR MEN
BIKER DESIGNS

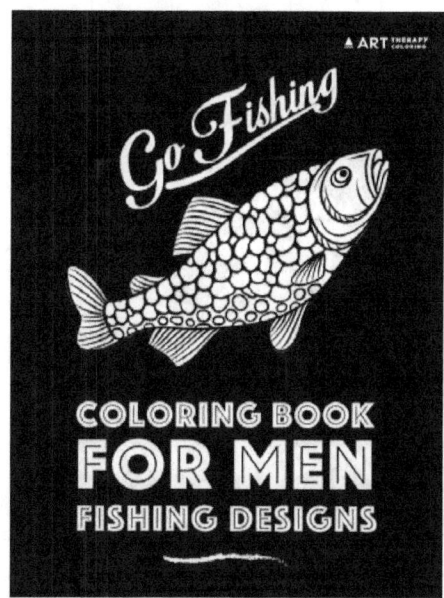

Go Fishing
COLORING BOOK
FOR MEN
FISHING DESIGNS

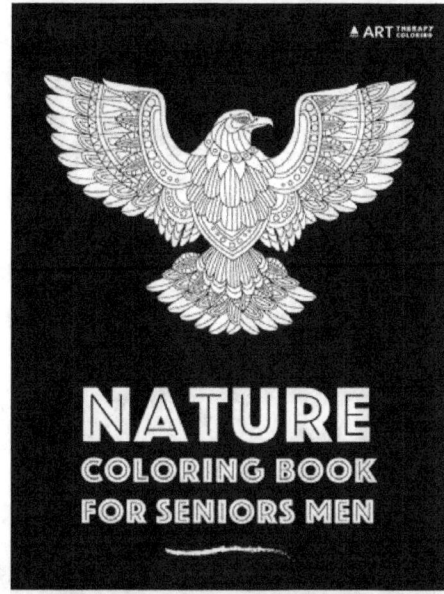

NATURE
COLORING BOOK
FOR SENIORS MEN

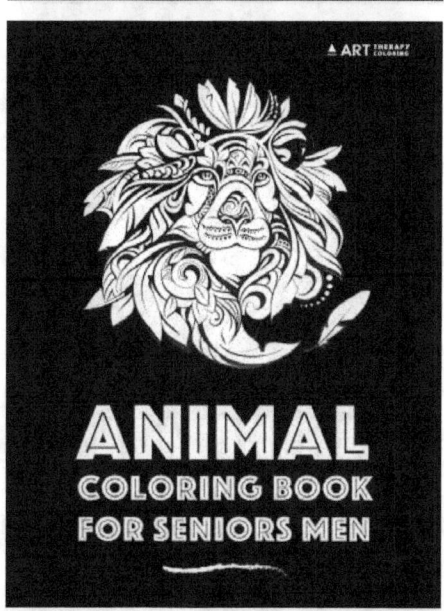

ANIMAL
COLORING BOOK
FOR SENIORS MEN

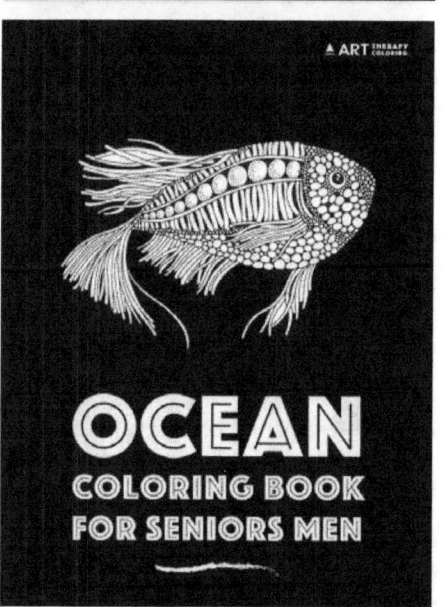

OCEAN
COLORING BOOK
FOR SENIORS MEN

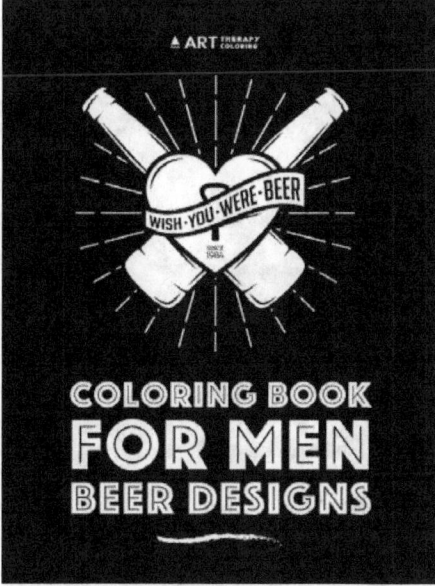

WISH·YOU·WERE·BEER
COLORING BOOK
FOR MEN
BEER DESIGNS

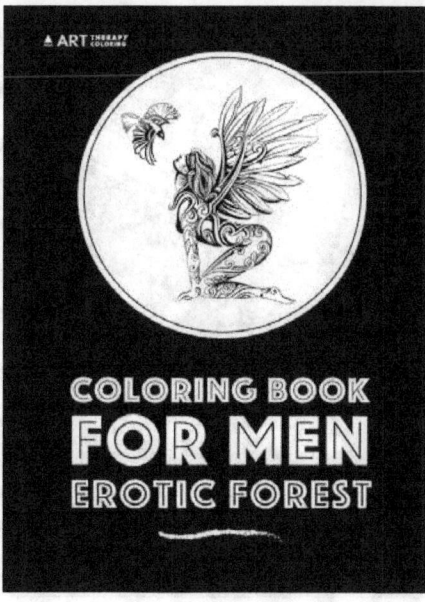

COLORING BOOK
FOR MEN
EROTIC FOREST

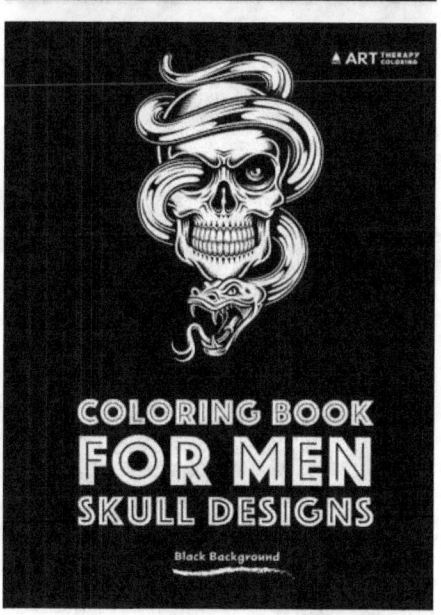

COLORING BOOK
FOR MEN
SKULL DESIGNS
Black Background

www.arttherapycoloring.com

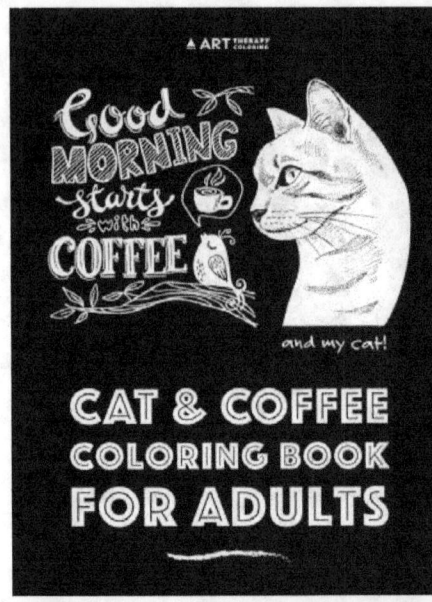

CAT & COFFEE COLORING BOOK FOR ADULTS

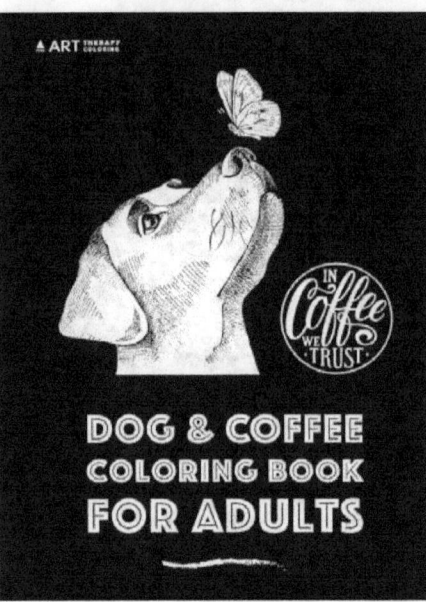

DOG & COFFEE COLORING BOOK FOR ADULTS

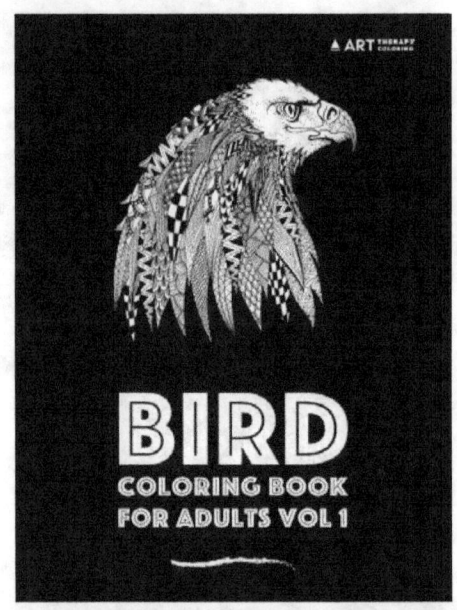

BIRD COLORING BOOK FOR ADULTS VOL 1

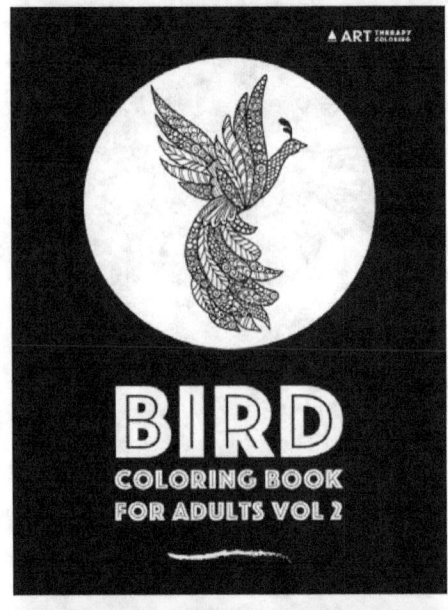

BIRD COLORING BOOK FOR ADULTS VOL 2

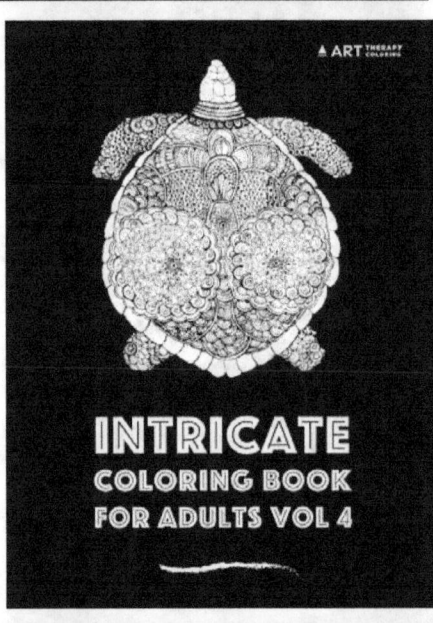

INTRICATE COLORING BOOK FOR ADULTS VOL 4

INTRICATE COLORING BOOK FOR ADULTS VOL 5

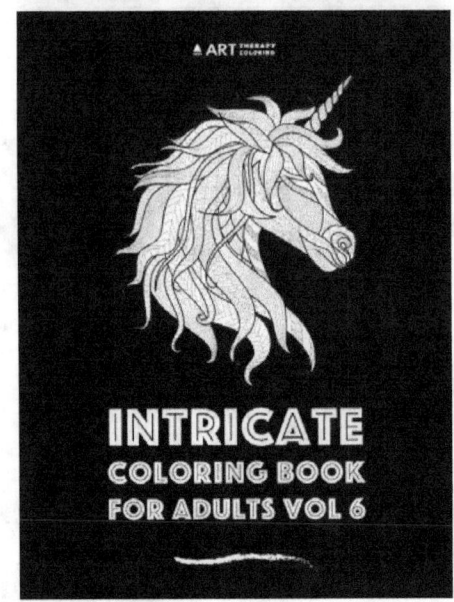

INTRICATE COLORING BOOK FOR ADULTS VOL 6

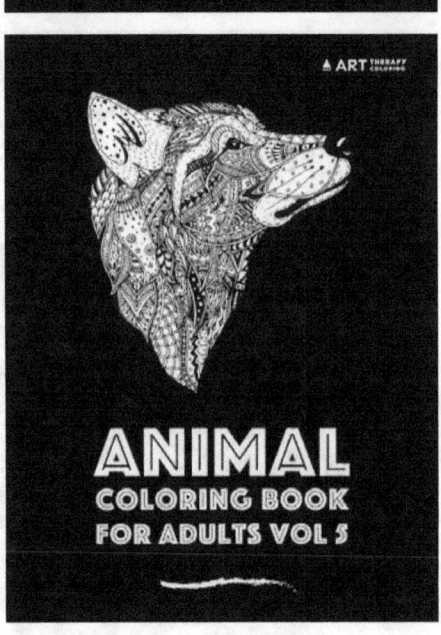

ANIMAL COLORING BOOK FOR ADULTS VOL 5

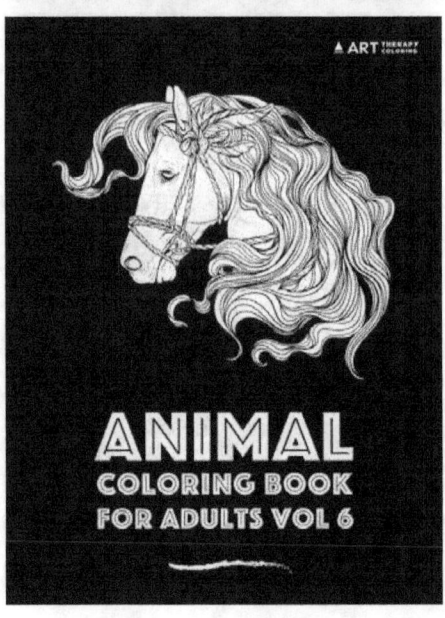

ANIMAL COLORING BOOK FOR ADULTS VOL 6

Art Therapy Adult Coloring Books

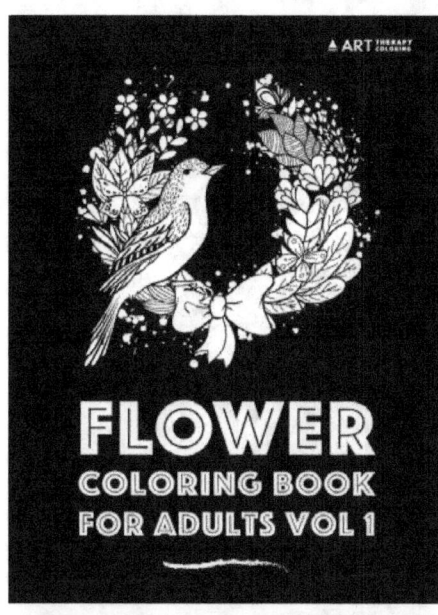

FLOWER
COLORING BOOK
FOR ADULTS VOL 1

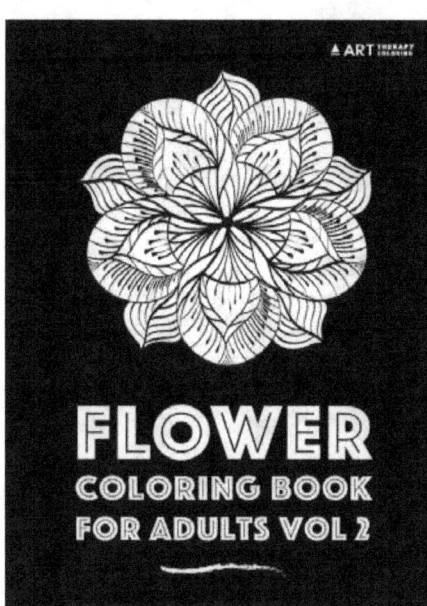

FLOWER
COLORING BOOK
FOR ADULTS VOL 2

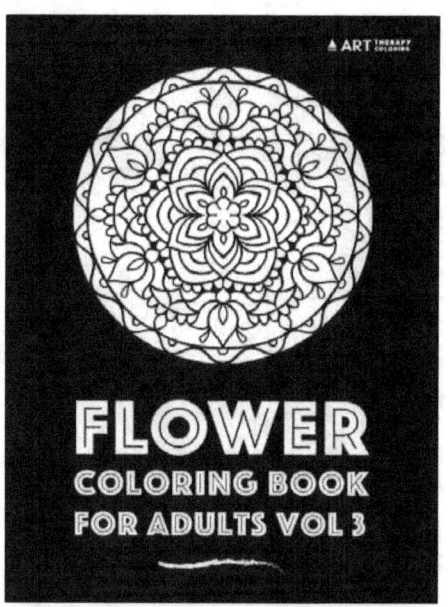

FLOWER
COLORING BOOK
FOR ADULTS VOL 3

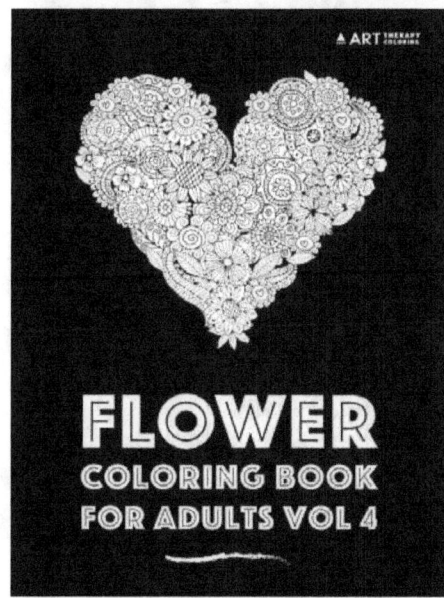

FLOWER
COLORING BOOK
FOR ADULTS VOL 4

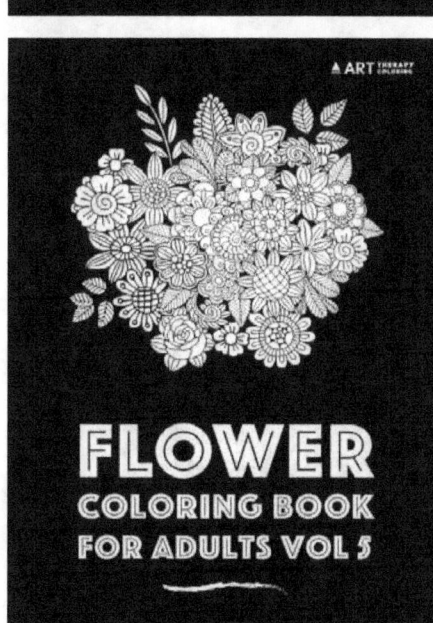

FLOWER
COLORING BOOK
FOR ADULTS VOL 5

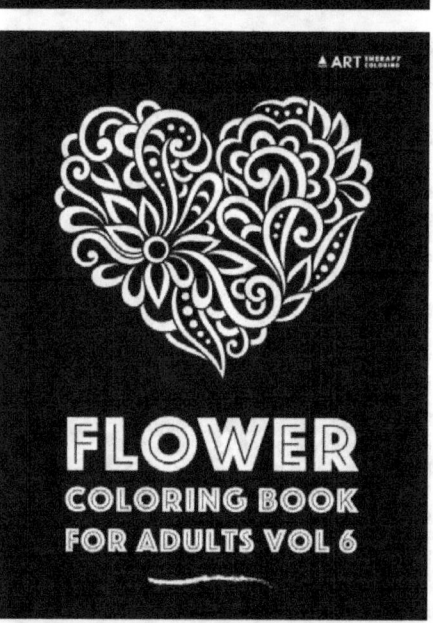

FLOWER
COLORING BOOK
FOR ADULTS VOL 6

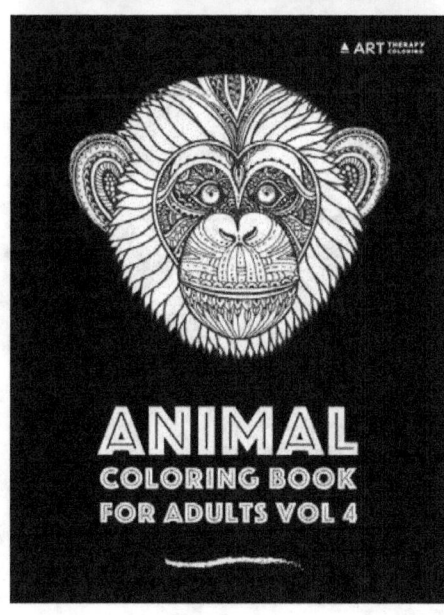

ANIMAL
COLORING BOOK
FOR ADULTS VOL 4

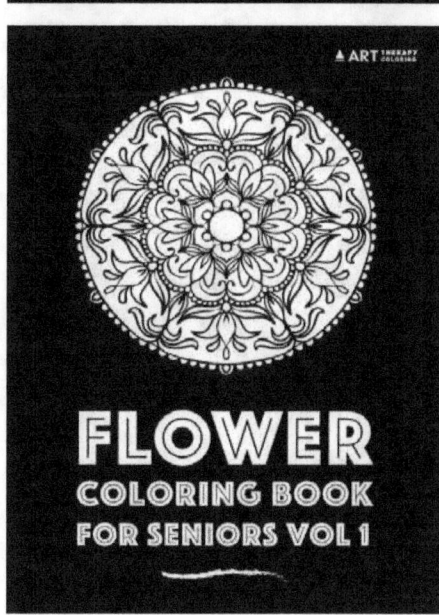

FLOWER
COLORING BOOK
FOR SENIORS VOL 1

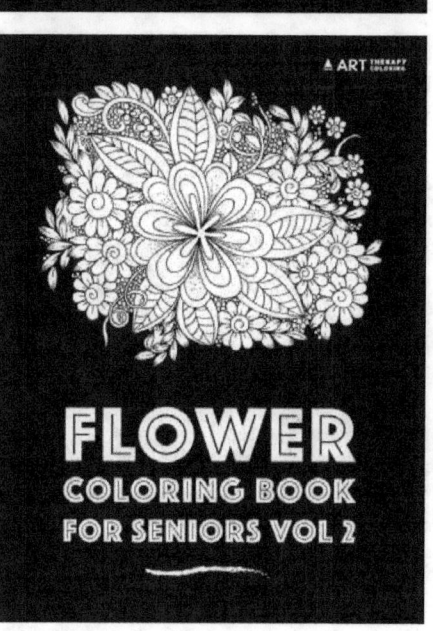

FLOWER
COLORING BOOK
FOR SENIORS VOL 2

www.arttherapycoloring.com

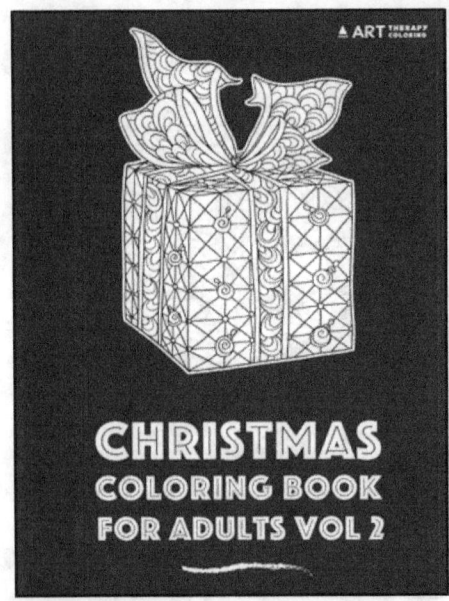

CHRISTMAS
COLORING BOOK
FOR ADULTS VOL 2

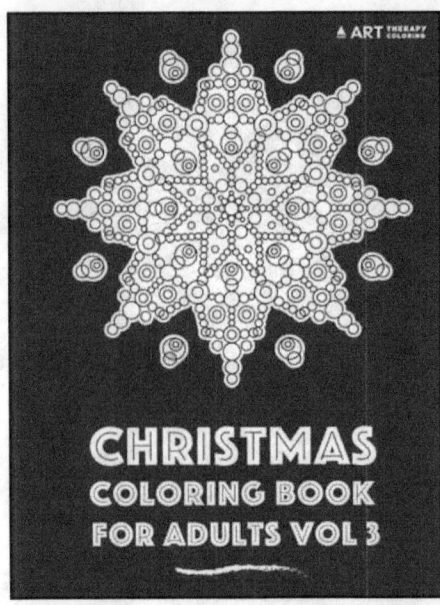

CHRISTMAS
COLORING BOOK
FOR ADULTS VOL 3

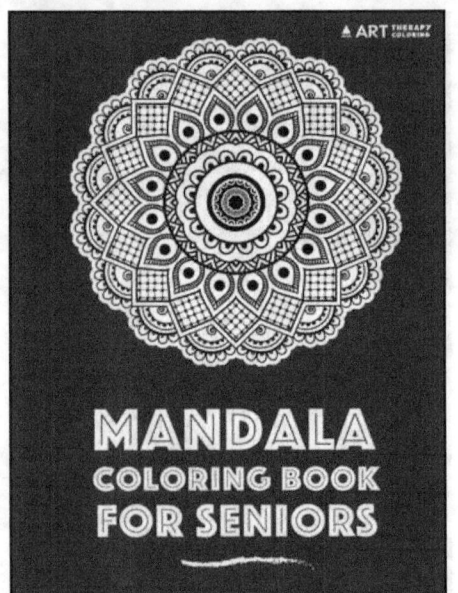

MANDALA
COLORING BOOK
FOR SENIORS

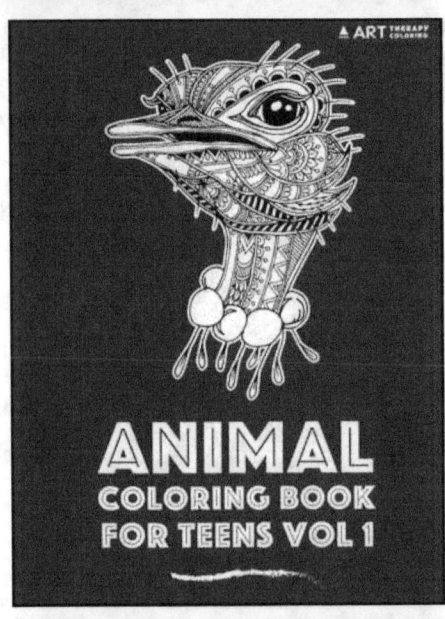

ANIMAL
COLORING BOOK
FOR TEENS VOL 1

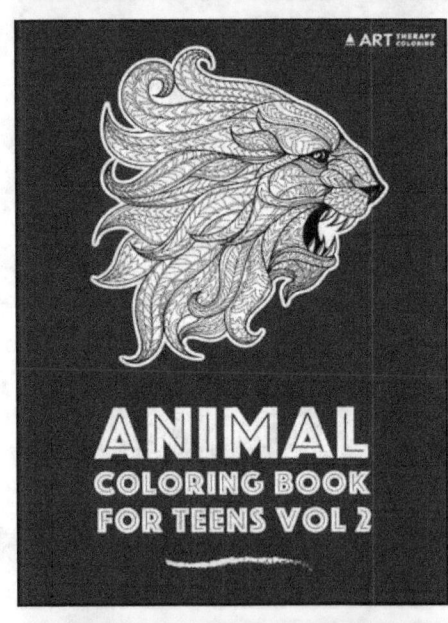

ANIMAL
COLORING BOOK
FOR TEENS VOL 2

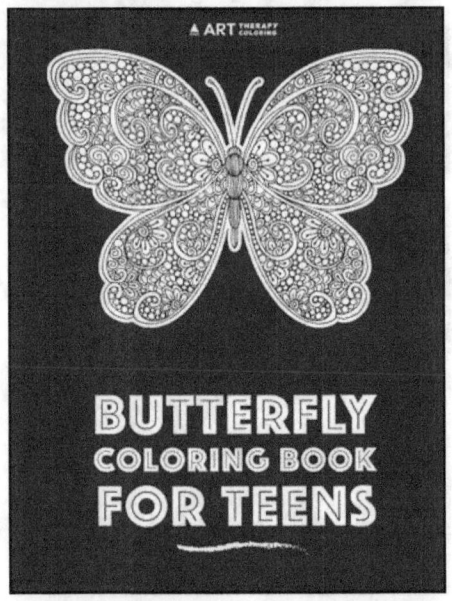

BUTTERFLY
COLORING BOOK
FOR TEENS

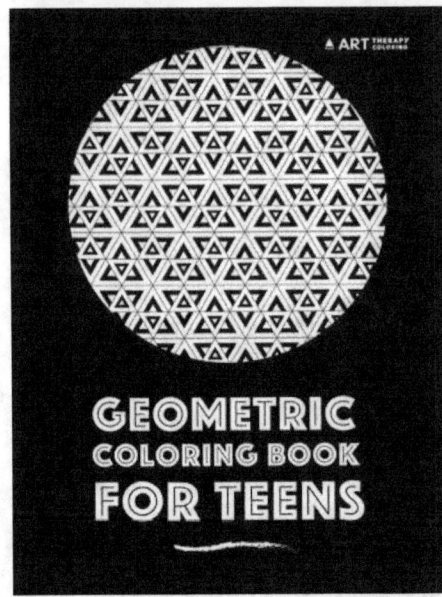

GEOMETRIC
COLORING BOOK
FOR TEENS

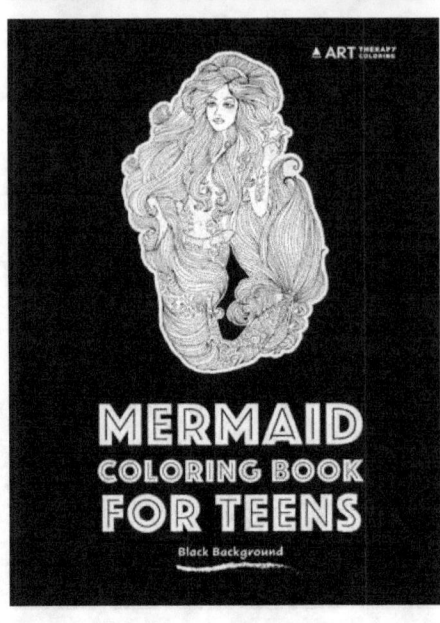

MERMAID
COLORING BOOK
FOR TEENS
Black Background

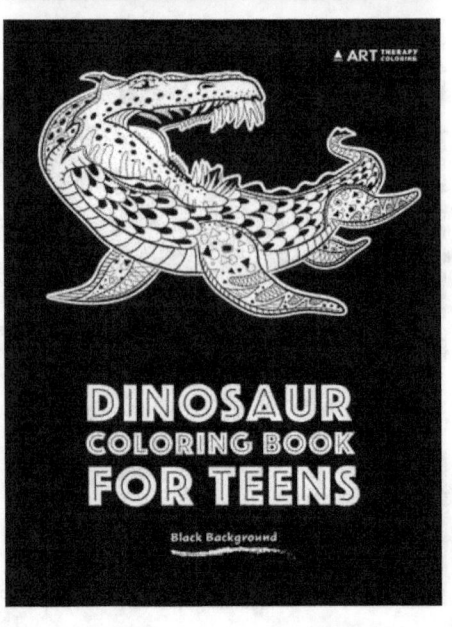

DINOSAUR
COLORING BOOK
FOR TEENS
Black Background

Art Therapy Coloring Books For Teens

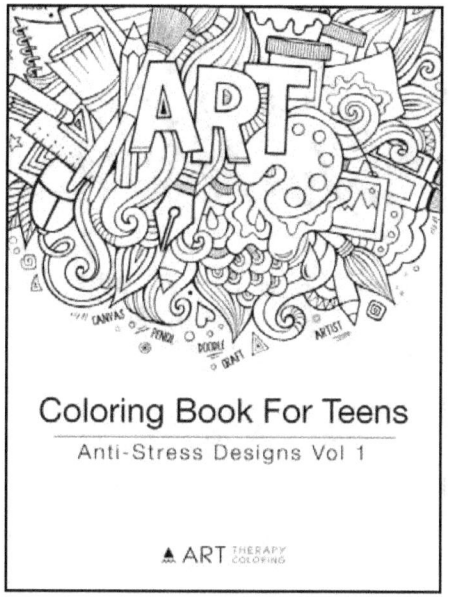

Coloring Book For Teens
Anti-Stress Designs Vol 1

▲ ART THERAPY COLORING

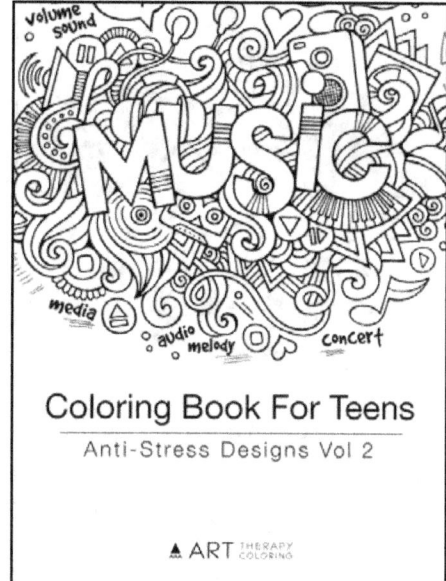

Coloring Book For Teens
Anti-Stress Designs Vol 2

▲ ART THERAPY COLORING

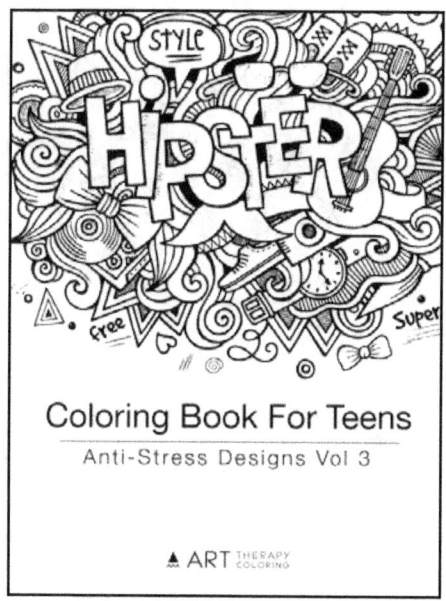

Coloring Book For Teens
Anti-Stress Designs Vol 3

▲ ART THERAPY COLORING

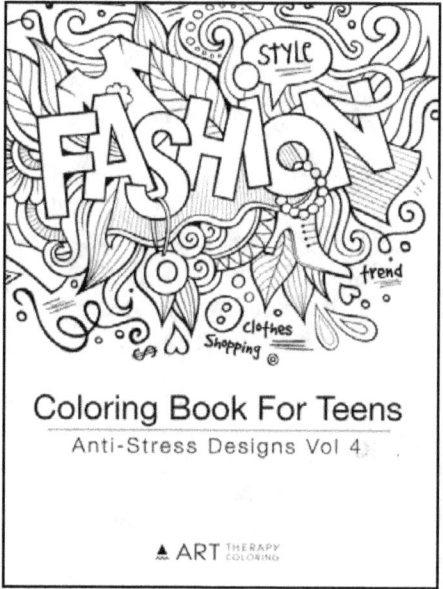

Coloring Book For Teens
Anti-Stress Designs Vol 4

▲ ART THERAPY COLORING

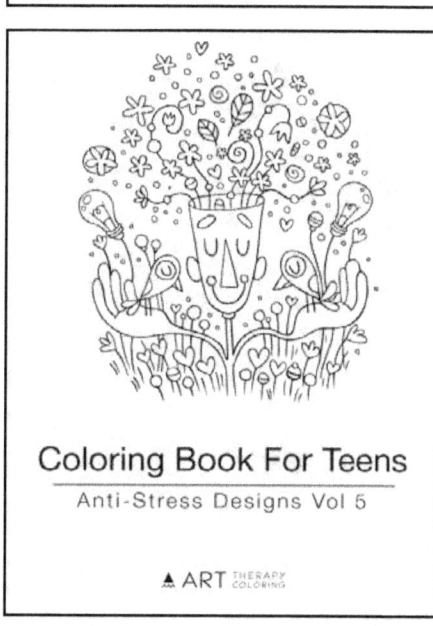

Coloring Book For Teens
Anti-Stress Designs Vol 5

▲ ART THERAPY COLORING

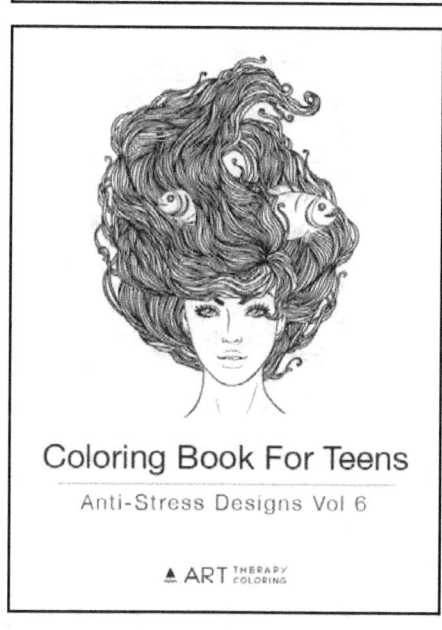

Coloring Book For Teens
Anti-Stress Designs Vol 6

▲ ART THERAPY COLORING

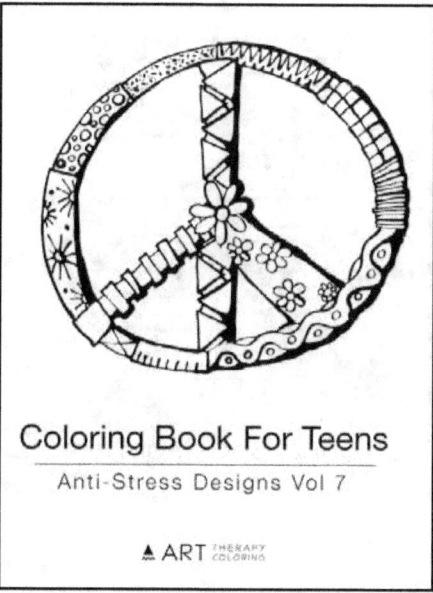

Coloring Book For Teens
Anti-Stress Designs Vol 7

▲ ART THERAPY COLORING

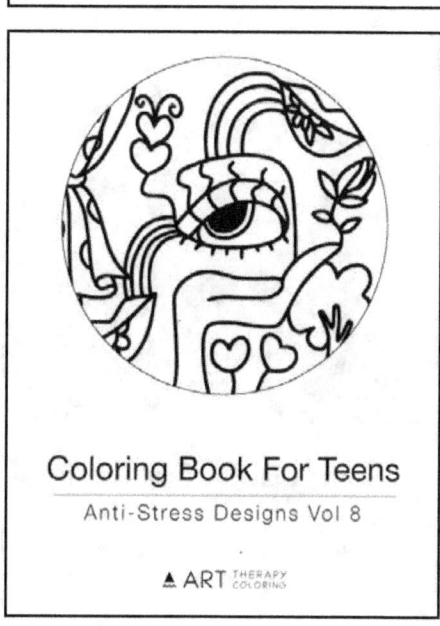

Coloring Book For Teens
Anti-Stress Designs Vol 8

▲ ART THERAPY COLORING

www.arttherapycoloring.com

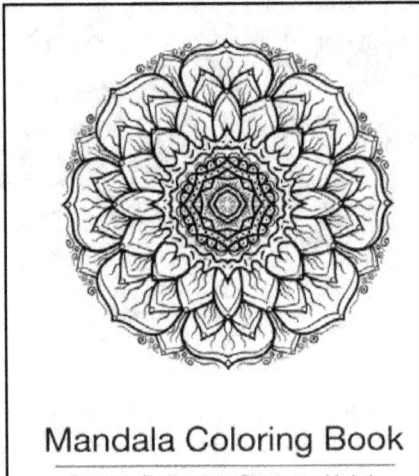

Mandala Coloring Book

Stress Relieving Designs Vol 1

▲ ART THERAPY COLORING

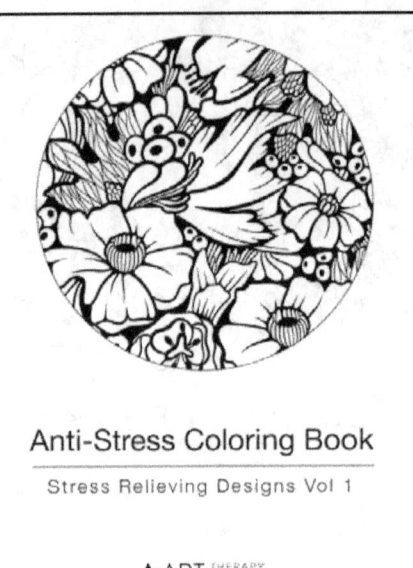

Anti-Stress Coloring Book

Stress Relieving Designs Vol 1

▲ ART THERAPY COLORING

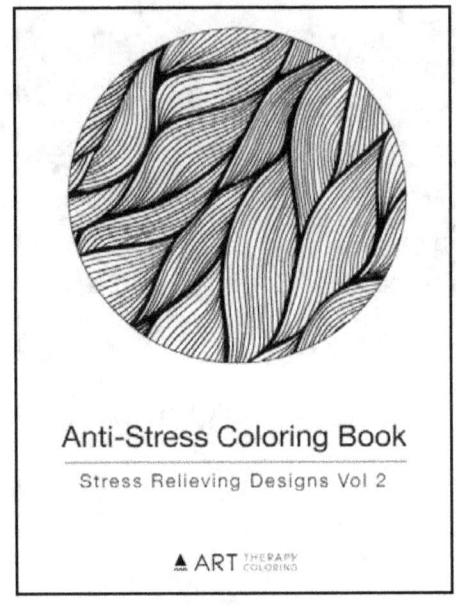

Anti-Stress Coloring Book

Stress Relieving Designs Vol 2

▲ ART THERAPY COLORING

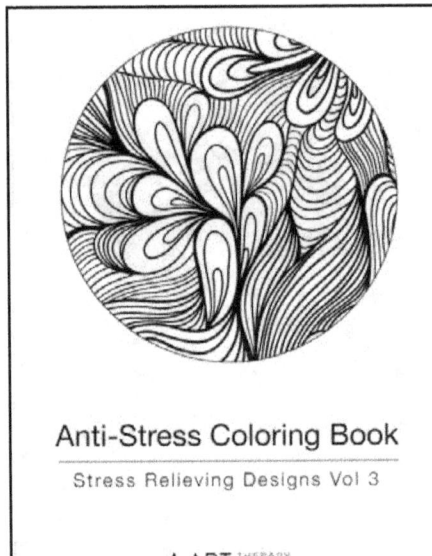

Anti-Stress Coloring Book

Stress Relieving Designs Vol 3

▲ ART THERAPY COLORING

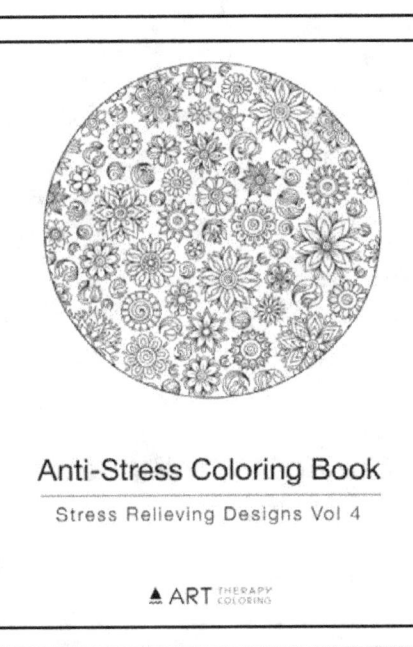

Anti-Stress Coloring Book

Stress Relieving Designs Vol 4

▲ ART THERAPY COLORING

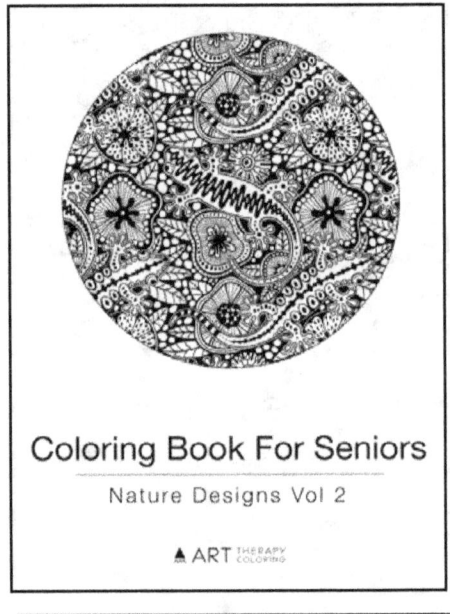

Coloring Book For Seniors

Nature Designs Vol 2

▲ ART THERAPY COLORING

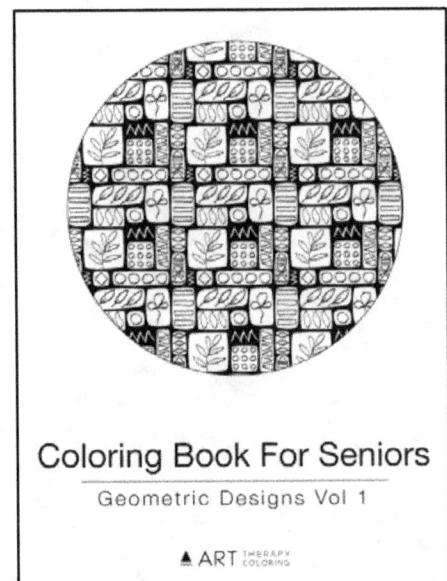

Coloring Book For Seniors

Geometric Designs Vol 1

▲ ART THERAPY COLORING

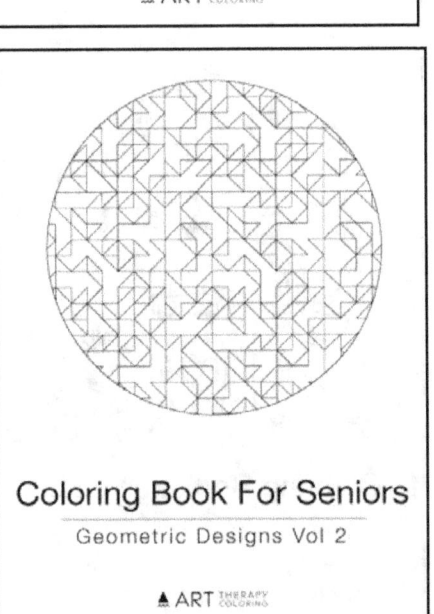

Coloring Book For Seniors

Geometric Designs Vol 2

▲ ART THERAPY COLORING

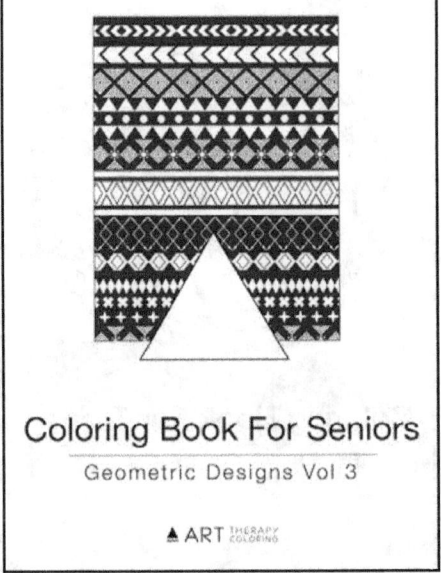

Coloring Book For Seniors

Geometric Designs Vol 3

▲ ART THERAPY COLORING

Art Therapy Coloring Books For Seniors

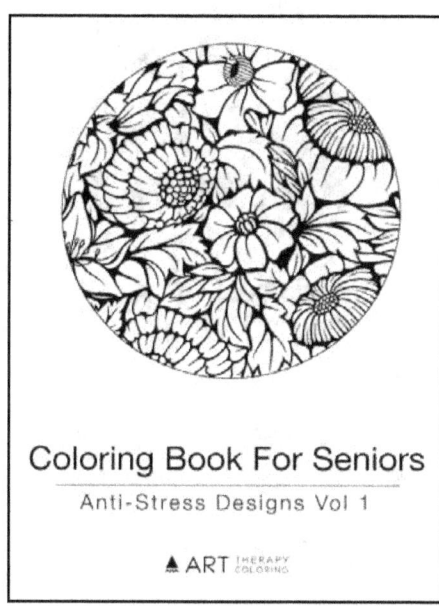

Coloring Book For Seniors
Anti-Stress Designs Vol 1

ART THERAPY COLORING

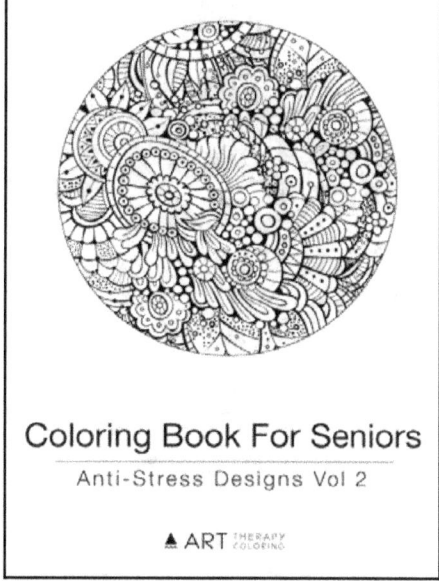

Coloring Book For Seniors
Anti-Stress Designs Vol 2

ART THERAPY COLORING

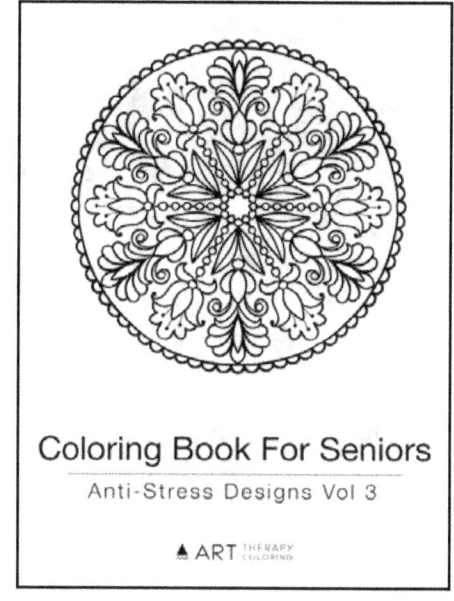

Coloring Book For Seniors
Anti-Stress Designs Vol 3

ART THERAPY COLORING

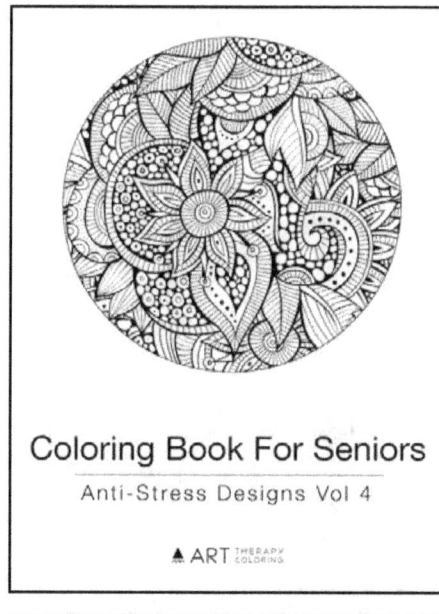

Coloring Book For Seniors
Anti-Stress Designs Vol 4

ART THERAPY COLORING

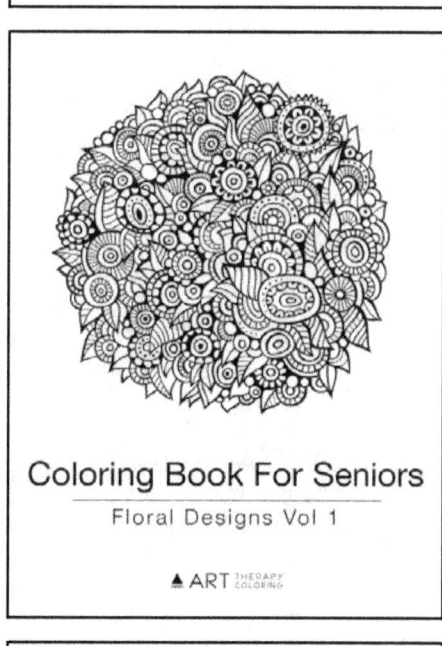

Coloring Book For Seniors
Floral Designs Vol 1

ART THERAPY COLORING

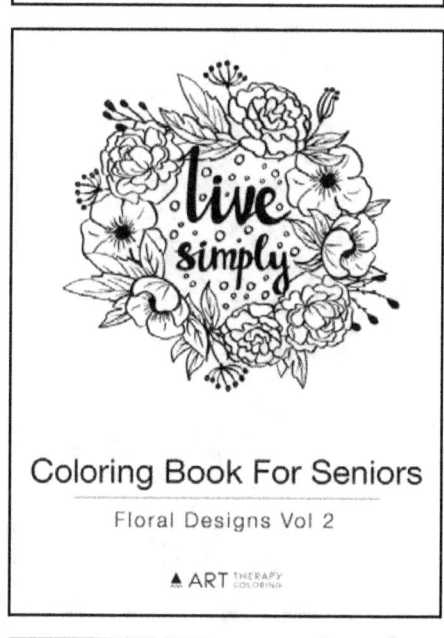

Coloring Book For Seniors
Floral Designs Vol 2

ART THERAPY COLORING

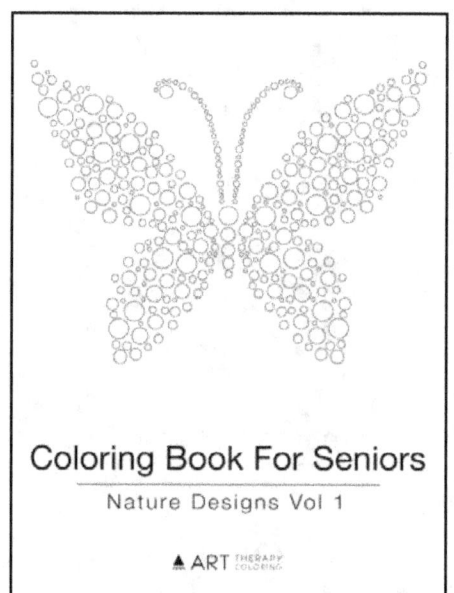

Coloring Book For Seniors
Nature Designs Vol 1

ART THERAPY COLORING

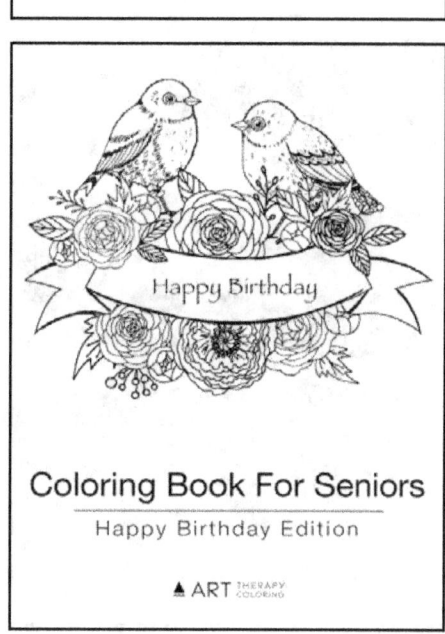

Coloring Book For Seniors
Happy Birthday Edition

ART THERAPY COLORING

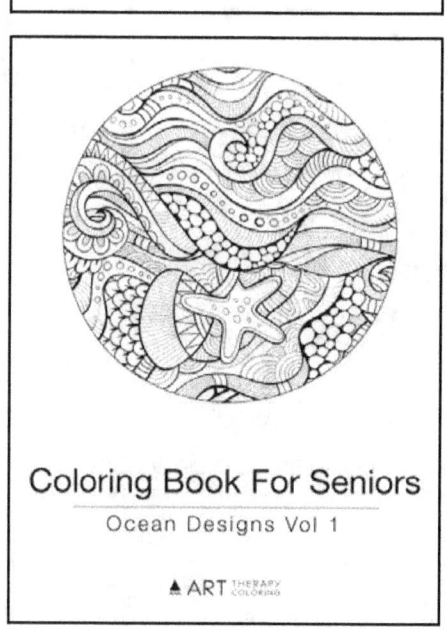

Coloring Book For Seniors
Ocean Designs Vol 1

ART THERAPY COLORING

www.arttherapycoloring.com

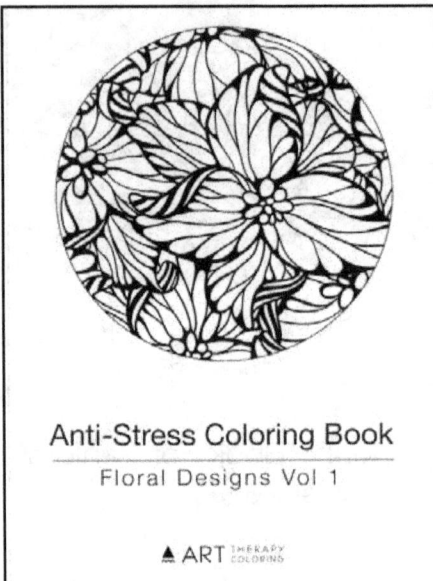

Anti-Stress Coloring Book

Floral Designs Vol 1

▲ ART THERAPY COLORING

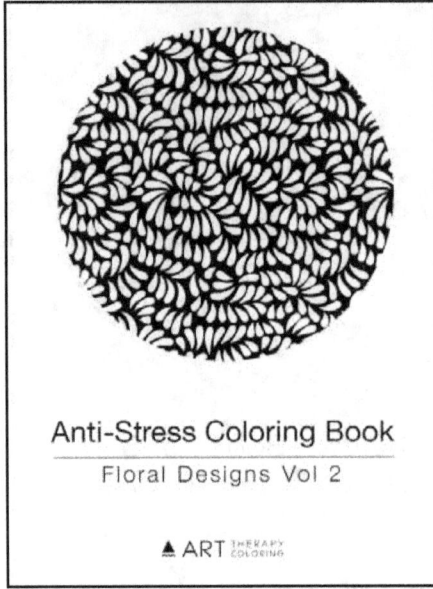

Anti-Stress Coloring Book

Floral Designs Vol 2

▲ ART THERAPY COLORING

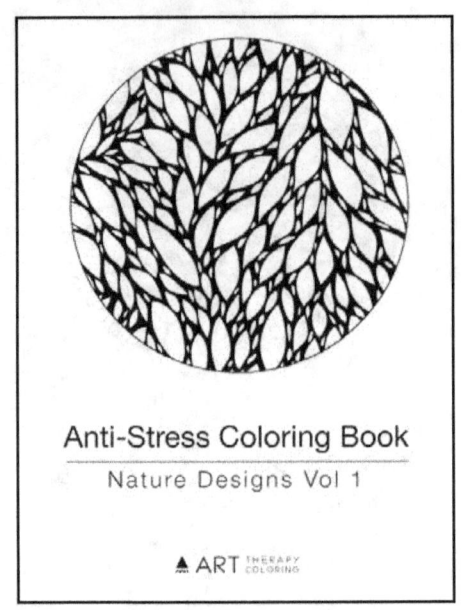

Anti-Stress Coloring Book

Nature Designs Vol 1

▲ ART THERAPY COLORING

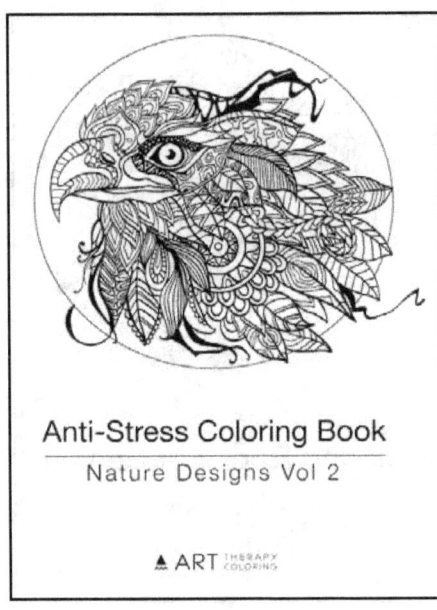

Anti-Stress Coloring Book

Nature Designs Vol 2

▲ ART THERAPY COLORING

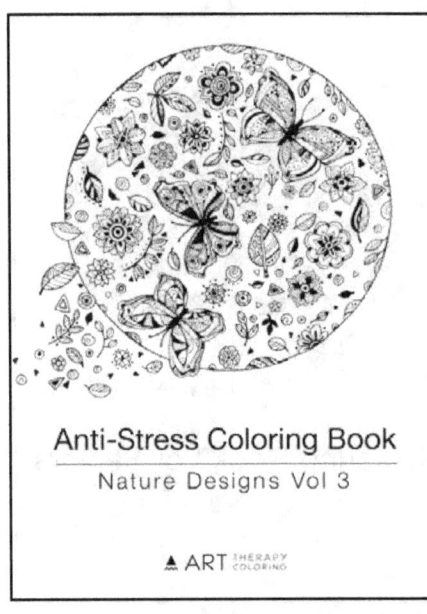

Anti-Stress Coloring Book

Nature Designs Vol 3

▲ ART THERAPY COLORING

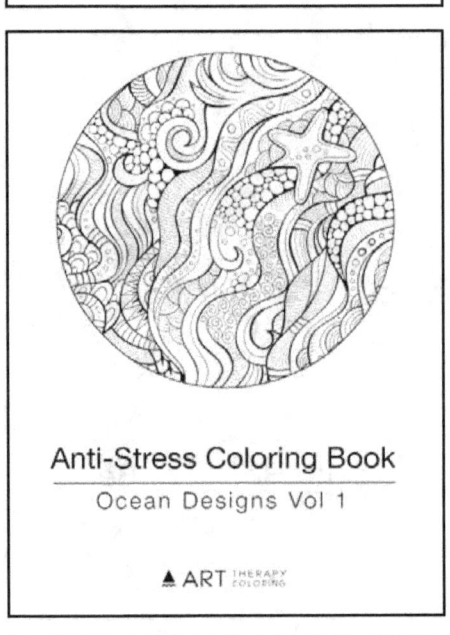

Anti-Stress Coloring Book

Ocean Designs Vol 1

▲ ART THERAPY COLORING

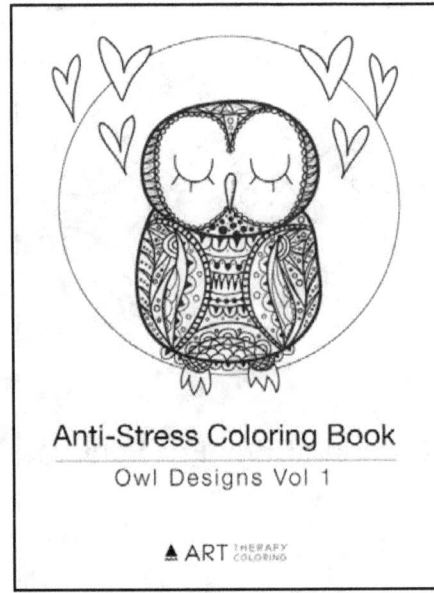

Anti-Stress Coloring Book

Owl Designs Vol 1

▲ ART THERAPY COLORING

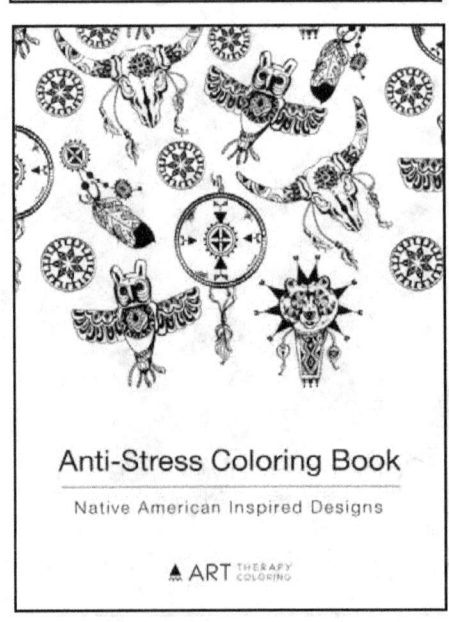

Anti-Stress Coloring Book

Native American Inspired Designs

▲ ART THERAPY COLORING

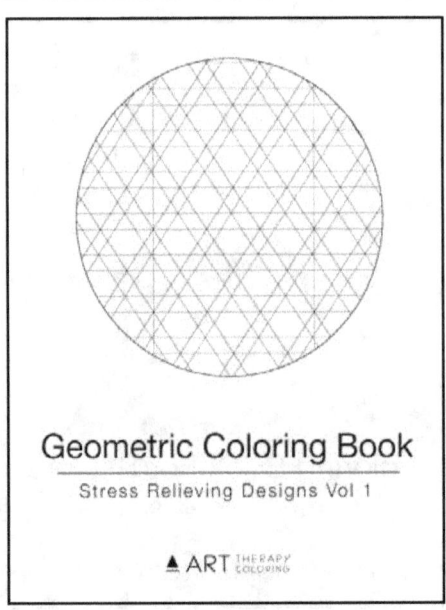

Geometric Coloring Book

Stress Relieving Designs Vol 1

▲ ART THERAPY COLORING

Art Therapy Adult Coloring Books

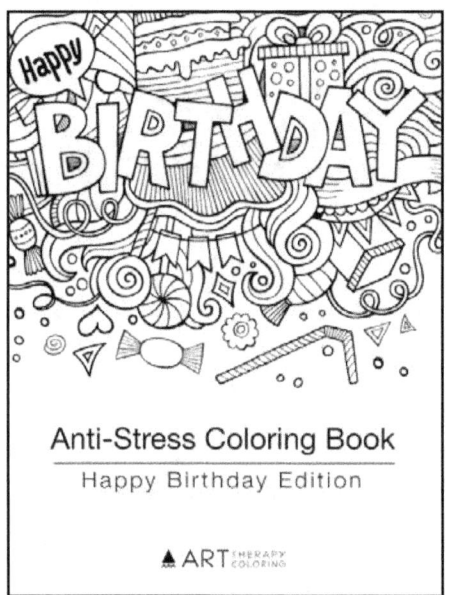

Anti-Stress Coloring Book

Happy Birthday Edition

ART THERAPY COLORING

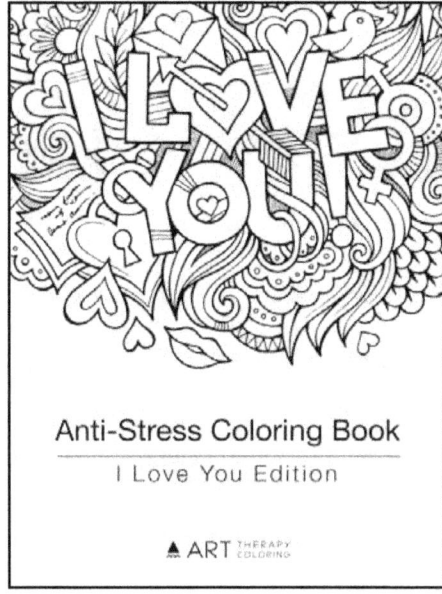

Anti-Stress Coloring Book

I Love You Edition

ART THERAPY COLORING

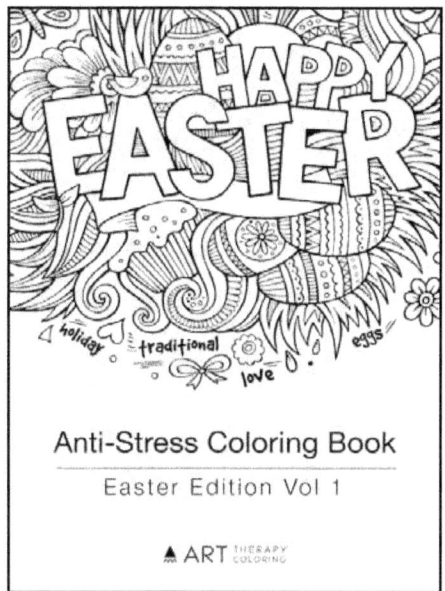

Anti-Stress Coloring Book

Easter Edition Vol 1

ART THERAPY COLORING

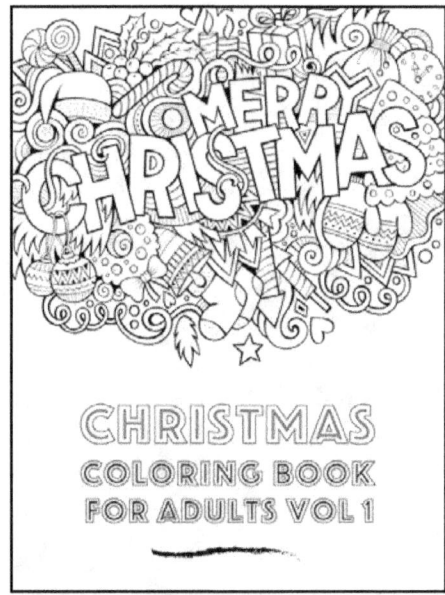

CHRISTMAS
COLORING BOOK
FOR ADULTS VOL 1

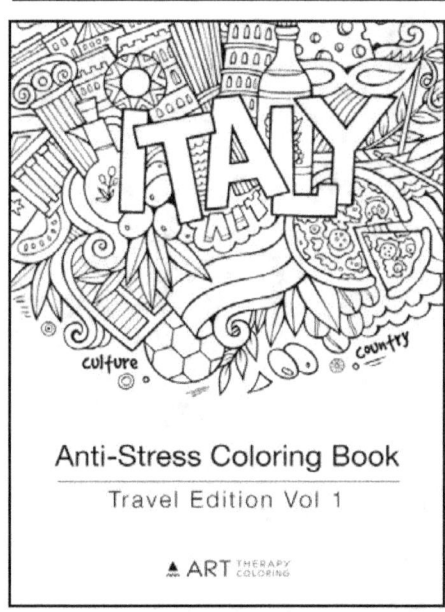

Anti-Stress Coloring Book

Travel Edition Vol 1

ART THERAPY COLORING

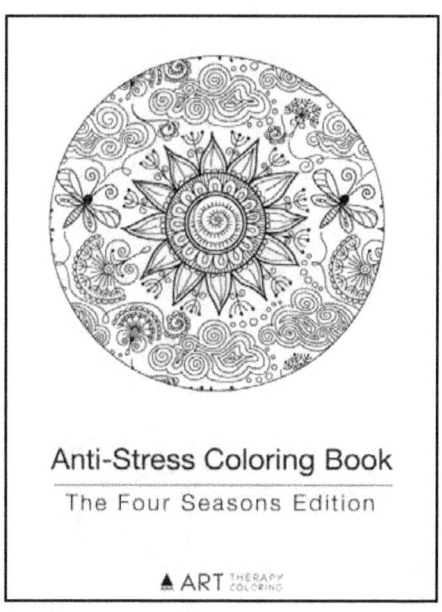

Anti-Stress Coloring Book

The Four Seasons Edition

ART THERAPY COLORING

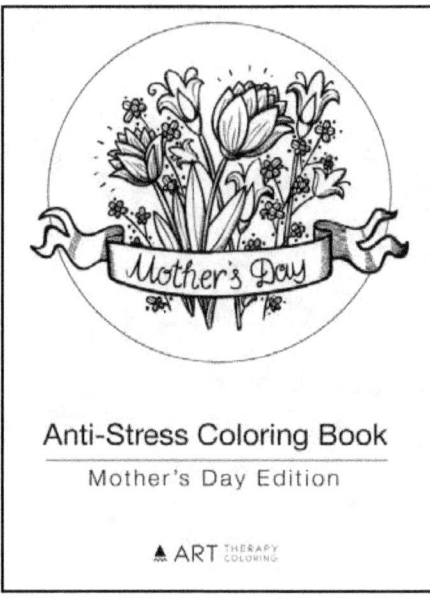

Anti-Stress Coloring Book

Mother's Day Edition

ART THERAPY COLORING

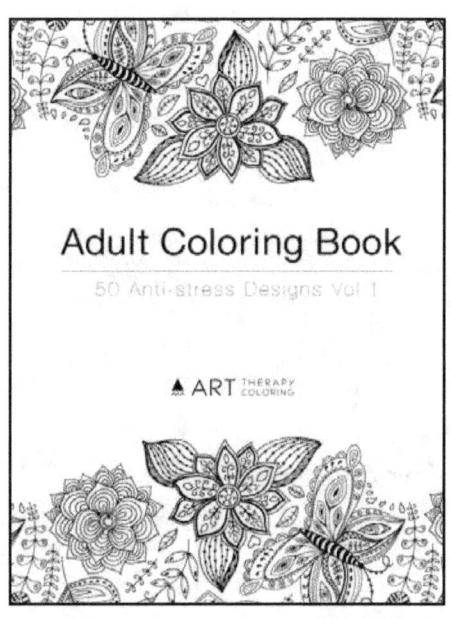

Adult Coloring Book

50 Anti-stress Designs Vol 1

ART THERAPY COLORING

Intricate Coloring Book
For Adults Vol 3

Published by:
Art Therapy Coloring
El Dorado Hills, California
www.arttherapycoloring.com

ISBN: 978-1-944427-63-4